The Teachings of Paul

The Teachings of PAUL

Mark E. Petersen

Deseret Book
Salt Lake City, Utah

© 1984 Deseret Book Company
All rights reserved
Printed in the United States of America
First printing May 1984

ISBN 0-87747-843-0
Library of Congress Catalog Card Number 84-70647

CONTENTS

Chapter One

A CHOSEN VESSEL

*A*S HE JOURNEYED to Damascus to persecute the Saints, a great revelation was given to Saul of Tarsus. The Savior personally appeared to him, a fact that lifted his call to one of major and unusual significance. Not only did he see the Lord at that time, but he conversed with Him.

Although Paul was sadly misdirected in his youth, his sincerity was beyond question. Therefore, as the light burst upon him and he heard the voice, he cried out from the depths of an honest soul, "Who art thou, Lord? . . . What wilt thou have me to do?" (Acts 9:5, 6.)

Throughout his persecution of the Saints, Paul loyally defended the Law of Moses, the only religion he believed. He felt that he did God service in protecting it from what to him was a threatening heresy.

Paul himself suggests this in his epistle to the Galatians: "For ye have heard of my conversation in time past in the Jews' religion, how that beyond measure I persecuted the church of God, and wasted it: and profited in the Jews' religion above many my equals in mine own nation, being more exceedingly zealous of the traditions of my fathers." (Galatians 1:13-14.)

The New English Bible rendering of this passage reads, "You have heard what my manner of life was when I was still a practising Jew: how savagely I persecuted the Church of God, and tried to destroy it; and how in the practice of our national religion I was outstripping many of my Jewish contemporaries in my boundless devotion to the traditions of my ancestors."

2 Paul recognized the light that struck him down as having come from heaven, and he instinctively seemed to know it was the Lord who spoke. So he addressed Him thus and asked for direction: "Who art thou, Lord? . . . What wilt thou have me to do?"

Here is seen the submission to heaven that had been instilled in him from childhood, and possibly even more so at the feet of Gamaliel, his Jewish teacher.

Violation of the laws given by Moses was a most serious offense toward God. This he knew. Certain sins brought even the penalty of death. Out of his great respect for the Law he responded to an urge to defend it. Out of that same respect, and especially from his devout fear of the Giver of that Law, now came his humble cry: "What wilt thou have me to do?"

In the Lord's dealings with mankind, He always communicates through living prophets. He told Amos that He will do nothing without such revelation. (Amos 3:7.)

Here was a case in point. The Lord did not exclude His prophet in this important event. Ananias was His instrument for this occasion. Coincidental with the manifestation that occurred on the highway, another revelation came, this time to Ananias in Damascus.

The Saints in the city knew well in advance that Saul was en route from Jerusalem to search them out and bring them to trial before the High Priests. This they feared, and especially was Ananias frightened. When the Lord instructed him to bring Saul into the city, he said:

"Lord, I have heard by many of this man, how much evil he hath done to thy saints at Jerusalem: and here he hath authority from the chief priests to bind all that call on thy name.

"But the Lord said unto him, Go thy way: for he is a chosen vessel unto me, to bear my name before the Gentiles, and kings, and the children of Israel: for I will shew him how great things he must suffer for my name's sake.

"And Ananias went his way, and entered into the house; and putting his hands on him said, Brother Saul, the Lord, even Jesus, that appeared unto thee in the way as thou camest, hath sent me, that thou mightest receive thy sight, and be filled with the Holy Ghost. And immediately there fell from his eyes as it had been scales: and he received sight forthwith, and arose, and was baptized." (Acts 9:13-18.)

There are important points to be noted here.

By revelation Ananias knew that the Lord appeared to Saul out on the highway. Also by that same revelation the Lord announced that Saul was a chosen vessel in His sight. This was the reason for the vision. Even before Saul was brought into the city, the Lord declared that this man would be His messenger to the Gentiles.

The revelation said further that Saul would testify before kings, which must have included both Agrippa and Festus and may have forecast his appeal to Rome. But he also was to preach to Israel. It was this assignment that led to his rejection by the Jews and his declaration that he would now go to the Gentiles.

"But when the Jews saw the multitudes, they were filled with envy, and spake against those things which were spoken by Paul, contradicting and blaspheming.

"Then Paul and Barnabas waxed bold, and said, It was necessary that the word of God should first have been spoken to you: but seeing ye put it from you, and judge yourselves unworthy of everlasting life, lo, we turn to the Gentiles. For so hath the Lord commanded us, saying, I have set thee to be a light of the Gentiles, that thou shouldest be for salvation unto the ends of the earth.

"And when the Gentiles heard this, they were glad, and glorified the word of the Lord: and as many as were ordained to eternal life believed. And the word of the Lord was published throughout all the region.

"But the Jews stirred up the devout and honourable women, and the chief men of the city, and raised persecution against Paul and Barnabas, and expelled them out of their coasts. But they shook off the dust of their feet against them, and came unto Iconium.

"And the disciples were filled with joy, and with the Holy Ghost." (Acts 13:45-52.)

There in ancient Damascus the Lord spoke to Ananias and gave him direction. The humble prophet obeyed without further objection.

4

When Paul reviewed this experience later in life, he added some important details. In defending himself from the vicious mob in Jerusalem, he said:

"And it came to pass, that, as I made my journey, and was come nigh unto Damascus about noon, suddenly there shone from heaven a great light round about me. And I fell unto the ground, and heard a voice saying unto me, Saul, Saul, why persecutest thou me?

"And I answered, Who art thou, Lord? And he said unto me, I am Jesus of Nazareth, whom thou persecutest.

"And they that were with me saw indeed the light, and were afraid; but they heard not the voice of him that spake to me.

"And I said, What shall I do, Lord? And the Lord said unto me, Arise and go into Damascus; and there it shall be told thee of all things which are appointed for thee to do.

"And when I could not see for the glory of that light, being led by the hand of them that were with me, I came into Damascus.

"And one Ananias, a devout man according to the law, having a good report of all the Jews which dwelt there, came unto me, and stood, and said unto me, Brother Saul, receive thy sight. And the same hour I looked up upon him.

"And he said, The God of our fathers hath chosen thee, that thou shouldest know his will, and see that Just One, and shouldest hear the voice of his mouth. For thou shalt be his witness unto all men of what thou hast seen and heard. And now why tarriest thou? arise, and be baptized, and wash away thy sins, calling on the name of the Lord." (Acts 22:6-16.)

Again here is testimony that Paul saw the Just One, Jesus Christ, and heard "the voice of his mouth." Once again, too, is recounted the nature of the call given him by the Lord: "I will send thee far hence unto the Gentiles." (Acts 22:21.)

By the personal attention He gave to Saul's call, the Lord

abundantly demonstrated the importance of His words to Ananias: "He is a chosen vessel." How did he become so? Certainly not while persecuting the Saints and putting them in jail. Could it have been elsewhere in some earlier time?

Jeremiah was chosen to be a prophet before he was born. (Jeremiah 1:5.)

Abraham was one of God's great leaders before the creation of the earth. (Abraham 3:23.)

Consider David, "a man after [God's] own heart." How and when did he become such? (Acts 13:22; 1 Samuel 13:14.)

Do men achieve giant soul-stature during their mortal lives alone? Or do they bring it with them from afar?

Noah was the angel Gabriel, serving in the presence of God in heaven. When did he reach his ascendancy? Surely not while building the ark and gathering beasts and birds to inhabit it.

Could a similar situation have existed with Paul?

Could it have been that his mighty soul had "risen from afar," possibly "trailing clouds of glory" as he moved into mortality "from God who is our home"?

To whom could Wordsworth's lines more aptly apply?

Did Paul sense this possibility as he wrote to the Ephesians? "According as he hath chosen us in him before the foundation of the world, that we should be holy and without blame before him in love." (Ephesians 1:4.)

When reclaimed from his youthful misdirection, even as young Alma, Paul blossomed into one of the grandest of all God's noblemen.

Chapter Two

TAUGHT BY
REVELATION

*P*AUL'S TEACHINGS were not the doctrines of men. His were the revealed truths of heaven, and it was by direct revelation that he spread the good word of the gospel. Said he to the Galatians: "But I certify you, brethren, that the gospel which was preached of me is not after man. For I neither received it of man, neither was I taught it, but by the revelation of Jesus Christ." (Galatians 1:11-12.)

This came as part of his rebuke to the Galatians in which he condemned the false teachings of men. The Galatians were in the path of apostasy, and Paul sought to recover them. Said he:

"I marvel that ye are so soon removed from him that called you into the grace of Christ unto another gospel: which is not another; but there be some that trouble you, and would pervert the gospel of Christ.

"But though we, or an angel from heaven, preach any other gospel unto you than that which we have preached unto you, let him be accursed.

"As we said before, so say I now again, If any man preach any other gospel unto you than that ye have received, let him be accursed." (Galatians 1:6-9.)

When writing to the Ephesians, he affirmed again that he was taught by revelation. (Ephesians 3:3.)

Addressing the Corinthians, he asked what would be accomplished unless "I shall speak to you either by revelation, or by knowledge, or by prophesying, or by doctrine?" And then he added: "For if the trumpet give an uncertain sound, who shall prepare himself to the battle?" (1 Corinthians 14:6, 8.)

He had warned the Saints before that the "time will come when they will not endure sound doctrine; but after their own lusts shall they heap to themselves teachers, having itching ears; and they shall turn away their ears from the truth, and shall be turned unto fables." (2 Timothy 4:3-4.)

Earlier he wrote Timothy on the same subject: "Now the Spirit speaketh expressly, that in the latter times some shall depart from the faith, giving heed to seducing spirits, and doctrines of devils; speaking lies in hypocrisy; having their conscience seared with a hot iron; forbidding to marry, and commanding to abstain from meats, which God hath created to be received with thanksgiving of them which believe and know the truth." (1 Timothy 4:1-3.)

He knew as Peter did that apostasy virtually stared them in the face. Said Peter: "But there were false prophets also among the people, even as there shall be false teachers among you, who privily shall bring in damnable heresies, even denying the Lord that bought them, and bring upon themselves swift destruction. And many shall follow their pernicious ways; by reason of whom the way of truth shall be evil spoken of. And through covetousness shall they with feigned words make merchandise of you: whose judgment now of a long time lingereth not, and their damnation slumbereth not." (2 Peter 2:1-3.)

It was Jude who gave additional warning: "But, beloved, remember ye the words which were spoken before of the apostles of our Lord Jesus Christ; how that they told you there should be mockers in the last time, who should walk after their own ungodly lusts. These be they who separate themselves, sensual, having not the Spirit." (Jude 1:17-19.)

Knowing all of this, and facing both the threat of Greek

philosophy and the idolatries and licentious persuasions of the Ephesians, true doctrine was important to Paul. He knew that salvation could come from none other.

The revealed word was the doctrine of Paul. He taught a religion now far different from that of the Jews and fully contrary to the pagan beliefs of the Gentiles. He knew there was only one way for him and the Saints to worship. He varied neither to the right nor left in his teachings. There could be no compromise with untruth. He followed nothing but the straight and narrow way, saying, "Henceforth there is laid up for me a crown of righteousness, which the Lord, the righteous judge, shall give me at that day: and not to me only, but unto all them also that love his appearing." (2 Timothy 4:8.)

Chapter Three

THE SUPREME TRUTH

*P*AUL HAD AN EYE SINGLE to the glory of God. His opening paragraphs in the epistles he wrote give ample evidence of this fact, not to mention his life of devotion. To the Romans he gave praise to God and Christ, together with his gratitude. (Romans 1:7-9.) He declared his love for the gospel in these words: "For I am not ashamed of the gospel of Christ: for it is the power of God unto salvation to every one that believeth; to the Jew first, and also to the Greek." (Romans 1:16.)

He thanked God for His grace in providing salvation, as he wrote to the Corinthians (1 Corinthians 1:2-4), and in his second letter he blessed the name of God for His mercies (2 Corinthians 1:3).

Hence he also said: "For this cause I bow my knees unto the Father of our Lord Jesus Christ." (Ephesians 3:14.) To the Galatians he did likewise. (Galatians 1:1-5.)

Again to the Ephesians he blessed both God the Father and Christ, His Son, for their grace in extending the gospel to them. (Ephesians 1:1-7.)

To Paul, the existence of God was the supreme fact of life. He spoke of both Father and Son. What was his understanding of the nature of God? Was He a personal Being, or was He some indescribable essence filling all the universe? Was Christ the physical Son of God, or is this concept but an

9

allegory? How could a drifting cloud or essence give birth to a human child? He knew that Christ was a person, but was His Father?

The entire gospel rests on a correct understanding of the nature of God. Can we appreciate the rest of the gospel if we are uncertain as to the Being we worship?

Paul taught with mighty power that Christ is the Son of God, but did he tell us about God also?

Two expressions in scripture are startling in their similarity, one spoken by the Savior, the other used by Paul in his letter to the Ephesians.

As Jesus emerged from the tomb on resurrection morning, Mary Magdalene was there, weeping for her Master. When she and the other women came on that first day of the week and found the tomb empty, she feared someone had stolen the crucified body. Then that touching scene took place wherein the risen Lord identified Himself to her.

As she realized that the resurrected Savior stood there before her, Mary attempted to embrace Him. Can we ever forget the words He spoke to her at that moment? He said, "Touch me not; for I am not yet ascended to my Father: but go to my brethren, and say unto them, I ascend unto my Father, and your Father; and to my God, and your God." (John 20:17.)

Amazing! Christ's Father—also the Father of the disciples! Christ's God—also the God of the disciples!

This was the Being Jesus referred to so often throughout His ministry. It was He to whom the Savior prayed and to whom we are taught to pray also.

Our Father—His Father.

Our God—His God.

It startles the mind to contemplate such great truths.

But Paul understood these facts and taught them in his ministry. Note his greeting to the Ephesians: "Grace be to you, and peace, from God our Father, and from the Lord Jesus Christ. Blessed be the God and Father of our Lord Jesus Christ, who hath blessed us with all spiritual blessings in heavenly places in Christ." (Ephesians 1:2-3.)

In clear, unmistakable language, this apostle distinguishes the Father and the Son as separate individuals— "*From* God our Father, and *from* the Lord Jesus Christ." Then he repeats that the Father is both "God and Father of our Lord Jesus Christ."

Is Paul's doctrine of Deity different from that of the Savior? In no way. It is identical. "My Father and your Father—my God and your God."

How appropriate, then, what he wrote to the Philippians: "Grace be unto you, and peace, *from God our Father, and from the Lord Jesus Christ.*" (Philippians 1:2. Italics added.) Two separate Beings!

When he wrote to the Corinthians, he opened his letter with the same words: "*from* God our Father, and *from* the Lord Jesus Christ." (1 Corinthians 1:3. Italics added.) Again, two separate Beings.

This concept appears in Paul's second letter to the Corinthians and in his epistle to the Galatians. (Galatians 1:3.)

When he wrote to the Colossians he gave thanks to the "God and the Father of our Lord Jesus Christ." (Colossians 1:3.)

And in addressing the Thessalonians he used "God *our* Father, and the Lord Jesus Christ." (1 Thessalonians 1:1. Italics added.) He repeated this phrase in his second letter to the Thessalonians. (2 Thessalonians 1:1-2.) Nor did he fail to do likewise in his letters to Timothy (1 Timothy 1:1-2; 2 Timothy 1:1-2), Titus (Titus 1:4), and Philemon (Philemon 1:3).

And did he withhold this doctrine from the Hebrews? Not at all! With them he was more explicit than ever. To them Paul declared that the Father is a *person* and that Christ, His Son, is a person also, His express image! (Hebrews 1:1-4.)

It becomes obvious that his understanding of the Deity was the universal doctrine of the church. There was no doubt as to the facts. The doctrine was basic and sound. God truly was the Father of Christ; both are persons, and man was made in their image.

Jesus constantly taught the Fatherhood of God, and on repeated occasions the Father spoke from heaven and declared Jesus to be His Son, with whom He was well pleased. (Matthew 3:17; Luke 9:35.)

But also, the Father was the God of Christ, the Being who was worshiped by the Savior. Jesus prayed to Him, obeyed Him continuously, and instructed all mankind to do the same. In prayer He taught: "After this manner . . . pray ye: Our Father which art in heaven." (Matthew 6:9.)

Is there a more convincing form of worship than to pattern one's life after another? Jesus not only worshiped his Father but also glorified Him in all He did. (Matthew 5:16; John 14:13; 15:8.) He kept His Father's commandments (John 15:10) and was taught by Him (John 15:15).

Not only did Jesus follow the pattern set by his Father, but He taught that it was a universal command for everyone. We should understand that "not every one that saith unto me, Lord, Lord, shall enter into the kingdom of heaven; but he that doeth the will of my Father which is in heaven." (Matthew 7:21.) Again he said: "For whosoever shall do the will of my Father which is in heaven, the same is my brother, and sister, and mother." (Matthew 12:50.)

There is this very illuminating instruction: "The Son can do nothing of himself, but what he seeth the Father do: for what things soever he doeth, these also doeth the Son likewise. For the Father loveth the Son, and sheweth him all things that himself doeth: and he will shew him greater works than these, that ye may marvel." (John 5:19-20.)

Two separate persons! One universal pattern of life!

No one should misunderstand the close relationship of Father and Son after considering these words:

"I can of mine own self do nothing: as I hear, I judge: and my judgment is just; because I seek not mine own will, but the will of the Father which hath sent me. . . .

"And the Father himself, which hath sent me, hath borne witness of me. Ye have neither heard his voice at any time, nor seen his shape. . . .

"Search the scriptures; for in them ye think ye have eternal life: and they are they which testify of me." (John 5:30, 37, 39.)

Jesus taught that God is our Father—that is, the Father of mankind. In supporting this doctrine, Paul taught that we are the offspring of God. Note this from Acts:

"Then Paul stood in the midst of Mars' hill, and said, Ye men of Athens, I perceive that in all things ye are too superstitious.

"For as I passed by, and beheld your devotions, I found an altar with this inscription, TO THE UNKNOWN GOD. Whom therefore ye ignorantly worship, him declare I unto you.

"God that made the world and all things therein, seeing that he is Lord of heaven and earth, dwelleth not in temples made with hands; neither is worshipped with men's hands, as though he needed any thing, seeing he giveth to all life, and breath, and all things; and hath made of one blood all nations of men for to dwell on all the face of the earth, and hath determined the times before appointed, and the bounds of their habitation; that they should seek the Lord, if haply they might feel after him, and find him, though he be not far from every one of us: for in him we live, and move, and have our being; as certain also of your own poets have said, For we are also his offspring.

"Forasmuch then as we are the offspring of God, we ought not to think that the Godhead is like unto gold, or silver, or stone, graven by art and man's device.

"And the times of this ignorance God winked at; but now commandeth all men every where to repent." (Acts 17:22-30.)

When he wrote to the Hebrews, Paul said: "Furthermore we have had fathers of our flesh which corrected us, and we gave them reverence: shall we not much rather be in subjection unto the Father of spirits, and live?" (Hebrews 12:9.)

And with further explanation, he told the Romans: "The Spirit itself beareth witness with our spirit, that we are the children of God: and if children, then heirs; heirs of God, and joint-heirs with Christ; if so be that we suffer with him, that we may be also glorified together." (Romans 8: 16-17.)

What then is man's destiny? Perfection—even like Christ. (Ephesians 4:13.) Was it not Jesus who taught: "Be ye ... perfect, even as your Father which is in heaven is perfect." (Matthew 5:48.)

Such is the Eternal Father of whom Paul taught, and such is His beloved Son, our Savior, our Redeemer. And such is man and the pattern of life he must follow.

Chapter Four

OUR SAVIOR AND CREATOR

*P*AUL TAUGHT most impressively that Jesus Christ was our Creator. He was especially emphatic on this point in his epistle to the Colossians. He begins this vital passage with his usual thanks to the Eternal Father "which hath made us meet to be partakers of the inheritance of the saints in light."

Still speaking of the Father, he then continues: "Who hath delivered us from the power of darkness, and hath translated us into the kingdom of his dear Son:

"In whom we have redemption through his blood, even the forgiveness of sins:

"Who is the image of the invisible God, the firstborn of every creature:

"For by him were all things created, that are in heaven, and that are in earth, visible and invisible, whether they be thrones, or dominions, or principalities, or powers: all things were created by him, and for him:

"And he is before all things, and by him all things consist.

"And he is the head of the body, the church: who is the beginning, the firstborn from the dead; that in all things he might have the preeminence.

"For it pleased the Father that in him should all fulness dwell." (Colossians 1:12-19.)

These verses are breathtaking in their description of Christ. Let us review them:

"In whom we have redemption through
his blood."

"Who is the image of the invisible God."

"By him were all things created."

"Is before all things."

"By him all things consist."

"The head of the body, the church."

"Who is the beginning."

"The firstborn from the dead."

"In all things he [has] preeminence."

"In him [shall] all fulness dwell."

Then was not Jesus divine in His own right? And is He not a separate individual by Himself, not of one substance with the Father, although made in the image of "the invisible God"? And was He not in the image of His mortal disciples also, since man was created in the likeness of God? Then is not God Himself a person, in whose image Jesus was made?

So here we have it from Paul, clearly and plainly stated. Jesus, the Son and physical likeness of the Father, is Savior, Redeemer, Creator, and first to be resurrected. And God the Father is a glorified Person, in whose "express image" is Christ.

Let us now look at the first chapter of Paul's epistle to the Hebrews. Here again is plain language, but it is startling to those who have not the truth.

That great letter begins: "God, who at sundry times and in divers manners spake in time past unto the fathers by the prophets, hath in these last days spoken unto us by his Son, whom he hath appointed heir of all things, by whom also he made the worlds; who being the brightness of his glory, and the express image of his person, and upholding all things by the word of his power, when he had by himself purged our sins, sat down on the right hand of the Majesty on high." (Hebrews 1:1-3.)

Again note the important points. Paul tells us that Jesus:
Came representing the Father, much as
the prophets had done before Him.

Is the Son of God, and the Heir of the
Almighty in all things.
Is the Creator through whom the worlds
were made.
Was "the brightness of [the Father's] glory."
Is the "express image" of His Father's *Person*.
Upholds "all things by the word of his power."
"When he had by himself purged our sins,
sat down on the right hand of the
Majesty on high."

What doctrine! What clarity! What an elevated understanding of the true Deity and of the relationship of Father and Son!

But this is not all, not by any means. Note in this epistle still another great declaration to those who sought a Messiah but did not recognize Him when He came among them. Paul here again portrays to the Hebrews the relationship between these two divine Persons. Speaking of the Father as referred to in the previous verses, he asked those Jews:

"For unto which of the angels said he at any time, Thou art my Son, this day have I begotten thee? And again, I will be to him a Father, and he shall be to me a Son?

"And again, when he bringeth in the firstbegotten into the world, he saith, And let all the angels of God worship him.

"And of the angels he saith, Who maketh his angels spirits, and his ministers a flame of fire.

"But unto the Son he saith, Thy throne, O God, is for ever and ever: a sceptre of righteousness is the sceptre of thy kingdom. Thou hast loved righteousness, and hated iniquity; therefore God, even thy God, hath anointed thee with the oil of gladness above thy fellows.

"And, Thou, Lord, in the beginning hast laid the foundation of the earth; and the heavens are the works of thine hands: they shall perish; but thou remainest; and they all shall wax old as doth a garment; and as a vesture shalt thou fold them up, and they shall be changed: but thou art the same, and thy years shall not fail.

"But to which of the angels said he at any time, Sit on my

right hand, until I make thine enemies thy footstool?" (Hebrews 1:5-13.)

There was certainly no doubt in Paul's mind about the true nature of the Godhead.

Paul spoke also of the Savior as the "Apostle and High Priest of our profession" (Hebrews 3:1), meaning Jesus, "who was made a little lower than the angels for the suffering of death, crowned with glory and honour; that he by the grace of God should taste death for every man. For it became him, for whom are all things, and by whom are all things, in bringing many sons unto glory, to make the captain of their salvation perfect through sufferings." (Hebrews 2:9-10.)

Now let us refer to another illuminating passage:

"Wherefore, holy brethren, partakers of the heavenly calling, consider the Apostle and High Priest of our profession, Christ Jesus; who was faithful to him that appointed him, as also Moses was faithful in all his house.

"For this man was counted worthy of more glory than Moses, inasmuch as he who hath builded the house hath more honour than the house.

"For every house is builded by some man; but he that built all things is God.

"And Moses verily was faithful in all his house, as a servant, for a testimony of those things which were to be spoken after; but Christ as a son over his own house; whose house are we, if we hold fast the confidence and the rejoicing of the hope firm unto the end."

Then Paul wrote, "As the Holy Ghost saith, To day if ye will hear his voice, harden not your hearts, as in the provocation, in the day of temptation in the wilderness." (Hebrews 3:1-8.)

In this connection he already had written the Corinthians, saying: "For the Jews require a sign, and the Greeks seek after wisdom: but we preach Christ crucified, unto the Jews a stumblingblock, and unto the Greeks foolishness; but unto them which are called, both Jews and Greeks, Christ the power of God, and the wisdom of God." (1 Corinthians 1: 22-24.)

How was Paul qualified to announce these truths with such power? Simply because he was a personal eyewitness of the Christ. He had seen the Lord and was personally taught by Him. Is not his own testimony acceptable? See what he said to King Agrippa:

18   "I verily thought with myself, that I ought to do many things contrary to the name of Jesus of Nazareth. Which thing I also did in Jerusalem: and many of the saints did I shut up in prison, having received authority from the chief priests; and when they were put to death, I gave my voice against them. And I punished them oft in every synagogue, and compelled them to blaspheme; and being exceedingly mad against them, I persecuted them even unto strange cities.

"Whereupon as I went to Damascus with authority and commission from the chief priests, at midday, O king, I saw in the way a light from heaven, above the brightness of the sun, shining round about me and them which journeyed with me.

"And when we were all fallen to the earth, I heard a voice speaking unto me, and saying in the Hebrew tongue, Saul, Saul, why persecutest thou me? it is hard for thee to kick against the pricks.

"And I said, Who art thou, Lord? And he said, I am Jesus whom thou persecutest. But rise, and stand upon thy feet: for I have appeared unto thee for this purpose, to make thee a minister and a witness both of these things which thou hast seen, and of those things in the which I will appear unto thee; delivering thee from the people, and from the Gentiles, unto whom now I send thee, to open their eyes, and to turn them from darkness to light, and from the power of Satan unto God, that they may receive forgiveness of sins, and inheritance among them which are sanctified by faith that is in me.

"Whereupon, O king Agrippa, I was not disobedient unto the heavenly vision: but shewed first unto them of Damascus, and at Jerusalem, and throughout all the coasts of Judea, and then to the Gentiles, that they should repent and turn to God, and do works meet for repentance.

"For these causes the Jews caught me in the temple, and went about to kill me.

"Having therefore obtained help of God, I continue unto this day, witnessing both to small and great, saying none other things than those which the prophets and Moses did say should come: that Christ should suffer, and that he should be the first that should rise from the dead, and should shew light unto the people, and to the Gentiles." (Acts 26:9-23.)

Our Savior and Creator

19

Chapter Five

THE CRUCIFIXION

*T*WO GREAT FACTORS were apparent in the Atonement of Christ, one His redemption on the cross, the other His resurrection. In the crucifixion the Savior paid the price of the sins of all who believe on Him. In the resurrection He broke the bands of death, came forth from the grave Himself, both literally and physically, and made possible a similar resurrection for all mankind.

What did Paul teach about the divine atonement?

Concerning the redemption on Calvary, he had much to say, even as he was eloquent in defense of the resurrection.

Let us ask first for whom Jesus died on the cross. Paul explains: "For all have sinned, and come short of the glory of God; being justified freely by his grace through the redemption that is in Christ Jesus: whom God hath set forth to be a propitiation through faith in his blood, to declare his righteousness for the remission of sins that are past, through the forbearance of God." (Romans 3:23-25.)

There we have the gospel story in but a few brief words. Who could have said it better or more precisely?

Paul wrote to Timothy that Jesus "hath saved us, and called us with an holy calling, not according to our works, but according to his own purpose and grace, which was given us in Christ Jesus before the world began, but is now made manifest by the appearing of our Saviour Jesus Christ, who hath abolished death, and hath brought life and immortality to light through the gospel." (2 Timothy 1:9-10.)

Paul found it necessary to warn the Ephesians of approaching apostasy, and in doing so he said:

"Take heed therefore unto yourselves, and to all the flock, over the which the Holy Ghost hath made you overseers, to feed the church of God, which he hath purchased with his own blood. For I know this, that after my departing shall grievous wolves enter in among you, not sparing the flock. Also of your own selves shall men arise, speaking perverse things, to draw away disciples after them." (Acts 20: 28-30.)

Note that he emphasized these words: "Which he hath purchased with his own blood." Significant!

Addressing the Ephesians further, and still speaking of Christ, Paul said: "In whom we have redemption through his blood, the forgiveness of sins, according to the riches of his grace." (Ephesians 1:7.)

To the Romans, Paul taught that "Christ died for the ungodly" (Romans 5:6), adding, "while we were yet sinners, Christ died for us. Much more then, being now justified by his blood, we shall be saved from wrath through him.

"For if, when we were enemies, we were reconciled to God by the death of his Son, much more, being reconciled, we shall be saved by his life. And not only so, but we also joy in God through our Lord Jesus Christ, by whom we have now received the atonement." (Romans 5:8-11.)

He told the Corinthians that "Christ died for our sins according to the scriptures." (1 Corinthians 15:3.) And he told Timothy: "For there is one God, and one mediator between God and men, the man Christ Jesus; who gave himself a ransom for all, to be testified in due time." (1 Timothy 2:5-6.)

He was equally plain with the Hebrews: "Though he were a Son, yet learned he obedience by the things which he suffered; and being made perfect, he became the author of eternal salvation *unto all them that obey him.*" (Hebrews 5: 8-9. Italics added.)

"The Author of Salvation"—that is why we call His plan "the gospel of the Lord Jesus Christ."

Most, if not all, Christians believe that the Lord died for us, of course, but their understanding of the doctrine of atonement varies widely from denomination to denomination, some of them stripping away the basic elements of His sacrifice. Thus they nullify the effect of His divine offering in what they teach and do.

All nonbelievers, of course, should know, and the various contending congregations must not ignore the fact, that Christ is not divided (1 Corinthians 1) and that, as Peter said: "Neither is there salvation in any other: for there is none other name under heaven given among men, whereby we must be saved." (Acts 4:12.)

Paul reflected this same truth when he taught Timothy that there is one God and one mediator between God and men, Jesus Christ (1 Timothy 2:5-6), forcefully recalling to mind his declaration to the Ephesians: "One Lord, one faith, one baptism, one God and Father of all, who is above all, and through all, and in you all." (Ephesians 4:5-6.)

No divisions in Christ? None whatever! There should be only oneness, a harmonious unity in Christ. Otherwise the structure crumbles.

Chapter Six

THE RESURRECTION

*P*AUL DEFENDED the fact of the physical resurrection of Jesus Christ with all the power of his zealous soul. To him, if there was no resurrection, there was no Christ. In a sense the two were synonymous in his mind. He vigorously challenged those doubting Corinthians:

"Now if Christ be preached that he rose from the dead, how say some among you that there is no resurrection of the dead?

"But if there be no resurrection of the dead, then is Christ not risen: and if Christ be not risen, then is our preaching vain, and your faith is also vain. Yea, and we are found false witnesses of God; because we have testified of God that he raised up Christ: whom he raised not up, if so be that the dead rise not.

"For if the dead rise not, then is not Christ raised: and if Christ be not raised, your faith is vain; ye are yet in your sins. Then they also which are fallen asleep in Christ are perished.

"If in this life only we have hope in Christ, we are of all men most miserable. But now is Christ risen from the dead, and become the firstfruits of them that slept." (1 Corinthians 15:12-20.)

Rebuking false ideas concerning the Fall of Adam, he wrote:

"For since by man came death, by man came also the

23

resurrection of the dead. For as in Adam all die, even so in Christ shall all be made alive. But every man in his own order: Christ the firstfruits; afterward they that are Christ's at his coming.

"Then cometh the end, when he shall have delivered up the kingdom to God, even the Father; when he shall have put down all rule and all authority and power.

"For he must reign, till he hath put all enemies under his feet. The last enemy that shall be destroyed is death." (1 Corinthians 15:21-26.)

This scripture harmonizes exactly with his declaration to the Romans:

"Wherefore, as by one man sin entered into the world, and death by sin; and so death passed upon all men, for that all have sinned: (For until the law sin was in the world: but sin is not imputed when there is no law. Nevertheless death reigned from Adam to Moses, even over them that had not sinned after the similitude of Adam's transgression, who is the figure of him that was to come. But not as the offence, so also is the free gift. For if through the offence of one many be dead, much more the grace of God, and the gift by grace, which is by one man, Jesus Christ, hath abounded unto many. . . .)" (Romans 5:12-15.)

Adam's sin was not to be canceled out by baptism. The original sin brought death as its penalty, and no action but resurrection could wipe it out, nothing but Christ's resurrection through which He extends resurrection to all the rest of us. Baptism was not involved in any way.

At death, do both body and soul descend into the grave, or are spirit and flesh separated by death?

Other sacred writers bring their explanations to sustain Paul. Solomon, as a case in point, wrote: "Then shall the dust return to the earth as it was: and the spirit shall return unto God who gave it." (Ecclesiastes 12:7.)

The example of Christ should set all doubts aside. His spirit did not sleep in the grave with His body. Neither did His spirit alone revive on resurrection morning leaving the body in the tomb, as some say concerning the resurrection of all others. Peter gives the answer, and it is clear:

"For Christ also hath once suffered for sins, the just for the unjust, that he might bring us to God, being put to death in the flesh, but quickened by the Spirit: by which also he went and preached unto the spirits in prison; which sometime were disobedient, when once the longsuffering of God waited in the days of Noah, while the ark was a pre- paring, wherein few, that is, eight souls were saved by water." (1 Peter 3:18-20.)

"For for this cause was the gospel preached also to them that are dead, that they might be judged according to men in the flesh, but live according to God in the spirit." (1 Peter 4:6.)

The spirits of the dead are alive and alert, and Christ visited them while His own body lay in the grave!

Resurrection, then, is a restoration of the spirit to the reanimated, purified body. As Paul explained, the corruptible flesh becomes incorruptible, the spirit returns to the renewed body from "God who gave it" originally, and death is "swallowed up in victory." (1 Corinthians 15:53-56.)

Then exultingly Paul said: "But thanks be to God, which giveth us the victory through our Lord Jesus Christ." (1 Corinthians 15:57.)

Why should anyone seek to discount the resurrection and say it is only half of what the scriptures teach? Why say it was simply and only spiritual?

When Paul said "corruption put on incorruption," he spoke of the mortal body as renewed, and when he said the mortal must put on immortality," he again referred to the physical body. Note his comparison with seed which is planted to produce new life:

"But some man will say, How are the dead raised up? and with what body do they come?

"Thou fool, that which thou sowest is not quickened, except it die: and that which thou sowest, thou sowest not that body that shall be, but bare grain, it may chance of wheat, or of some other grain: but God giveth it a body as it hath pleased him, and to every seed his own body." (1 Corinthians 15:35-38.)

Yes, as he truly said: "So also is the resurrection of the dead. It is sown in corruption; it is raised in incorruption: it is sown in dishonour; it is raised in glory: it is sown in weakness; it is raised in power: it is sown a natural body; it is raised a spiritual body. There is a natural body, and there is a spiritual body." (1 Corinthians 15:42-44.) But it is still "the body" and not just the spirit alone.

Was the Lord's resurrection physical? Did Adam die physically? Don't we all die physically? And what overcomes this physical death? Only a physical resurrection! Nothing else! Jesus Himself declared that His own resurrection was physical. (Luke 24:39-43; John 20:24-28.)

Of this Paul testified: "Brethren, I declare unto you the gospel which I preached unto you, which also ye have received, and wherein ye stand; by which also ye are saved, if ye keep in memory what I preached unto you, unless ye have believed in vain.

"For I delivered unto you first of all that which I also received, how that Christ died for our sins according to the scriptures; and that he was buried, and that he rose again the third day according to the scriptures: and that he was seen of Cephas, then of the twelve: after that, he was seen of above five hundred brethren at once; of whom the greater part remain unto this present, but some are fallen asleep.

"After that, he was seen of James; then of all the apostles.

"And last of all he was seen of me also, as of one born out of due time." (1 Corinthians 15:1-8.)

Paul was an eyewitness!

The Romans were told: "Who is he that condemneth? It is Christ that died, yea rather, that is risen again, who is even at the right hand of God, who also maketh intercession for us." (Romans 8:34.) To this Paul added: "For to this end Christ both died, and rose, and revived, that he might be Lord both of the dead and living." (Romans 14:9.)

Speaking of a universal resurrection, Paul wrote that God "will also raise up us by his own power." (1 Corinthians 6:14. See also 2 Corinthians 4:14.)

He taught the Philippians: "For our conversation is in heaven; from whence also we look for the Saviour, the Lord Jesus Christ: Who shall change *our vile body, that it may be fashioned like unto his glorious body,* according to the work-

ing whereby he is able even to subdue all things unto himself." (Philippians 3:20-21. Italics added.)

Yes, our bodies—our physical bodies—though vile and corruptible now will be "fashioned like unto his glorious body." That means nothing less than a physical resurrection!

Paul described the resurrection to the Thessalonians like this: "The Lord himself shall descend from heaven with a shout, with the voice of the archangel, and with the trump of God: and the dead in Christ shall rise first: then we which are alive and remain shall be caught up together with them in the clouds, to meet the Lord in the air: and so shall we ever be with the Lord." (1 Thessalonians 4:16-17.)

Paul's whole treatise on the resurrection is well supported by other biblical writers. Isaiah, for example, wrote: "Thy dead men shall live, together with my dead body shall they arise. Awake and sing, ye that dwell in dust: for thy dew is as the dew of herbs, and the earth shall cast out the dead." (Isaiah 26:19.)

Can anything be more specific concerning the physical nature of the resurrection than what Ezekiel wrote: "Prophesy and say unto [Israel], Thus saith the Lord God; Behold, O my people, I will open your graves, and cause you to come up out of your graves, and bring you into the land of Israel. And ye shall know that I am the Lord, when I have opened your graves, O my people, and brought you up out of your graves." (Ezekiel 37:12-13.)

Chapter Seven

THE LORD'S SUPPER

*T*HE SACRAMENT of the Lord's Supper is a major proof of the physical nature of Christ's atonement. Preceding His passion, the Lord met with His twelve and they ate the passover supper together.

It was on this night that Judas made his final arrangement to betray Jesus. Previously he had gone to the high priests to bargain with them. The record says: "One of the twelve, called Judas Iscariot, went unto the chief priests, and said unto them, What will ye give me, and I will deliver him unto you? And they covenanted with him for thirty pieces of silver. And from that time he sought opportunity to betray him."

The disciples sensed something unusual as they ate the Passover with the Master. They "did as Jesus had appointed them; and they made ready the passover. Now when the even was come, he sat down with the twelve."

Then it was that Jesus made the startling announcement: "Verily I say unto you, that one of you shall betray me."

Eleven of them, in deep sorrow, asked, "Is it I?"

"And he answered and said, He that dippeth his hand with me in the dish, the same shall betray me. The Son of man goeth as it is written of him: but woe unto that man by whom the Son of man is betrayed! it had been good for that man if he had not been born."

Then Judas asked, "Master, is it I?" And the Lord replied,
"Thou hast said." (Matthew 26:14-25.)

Luke records that "then entered Satan into Judas surnamed Iscariot, being of the number of the twelve. And he
went his way, and communed with the chief priests and cap-
tains, how he might betray him unto them. And they were
glad, and covenanted to give him money. And he promised,
and sought opportunity to betray him unto them in the ab-
sence of the multitude." (Luke 22:3-6.)

It will be remembered that the Lord, still at the table,
took bread and blessed it and broke it. Then He asked the disciples to eat of it in remembrance of His body, which soon
would be crucified. They also drank of the proffered cup, in
remembrance of His blood, to be shed on Calvary.

He thus made as clear as could be the physical nature of
His sacrifice. His body and His blood! The entire process was
a physical one that had supreme significance spiritually,
being so directly related to our salvation. Its important meaning remains with us to this day, undiminished.

Without His sacrifice there would be no salvation. This
great fact must never be forgotten. Jesus gave us this sacra-
mental ordinance that we might always remember Him, the
sacrificial Lamb of God, and remember also to keep His commandments. If we do not obey, can we say we remember
Him?

Since the sacrament of the Lord's Supper is such a vital
part of our religion, what did Paul have to say about it? He
knew that Christ died physically on the cross. He also knew
that the resurrection of Jesus was physical—one of flesh and
bones. (Luke 24:36-43.) And He knew that the bread and
drink that the Savior blessed and gave to the brethren were
also physical. He had been given this knowledge by revelation. Note his words as he described the Last Supper to the
Corinthians:

"I have received of the Lord that which also I delivered
unto you, That the Lord Jesus the same night in which he was
betrayed took bread: and when he had given thanks, he brake
it, and said, Take, eat: this is my body, which is broken for you:
this do in remembrance of me.

"After the same manner also he took the cup, when he had supped, saying, This cup is the new testament in my blood: this do ye, as oft as ye drink it, in remembrance of me.

"For as often as ye eat this bread, and drink this cup, ye do shew the Lord's death till he come." (1 Corinthians 11:23-26.)

Paul made it clear that there were two parts to the sacrament, the broken bread and the cup. Neither is complete without the other. The two were emphasized by Paul even as the Savior had done on the night He instituted the sacrament. Administration of only one emblem to congregations of Christians is a departure from the Lord's original pattern.

Paul emphasized, as did the Savior, that these emblems were to be administered separately as a reminder of the crucifixion of Christ's body, adding: "For as often as ye eat this bread, and drink this cup, ye do shew the Lord's death till he come." (1 Corinthians 11:26.)

When he referred to the sacrament in an earlier chapter, he said: "The cup of blessing which we bless, is it not the communion of the blood of Christ? The bread which we break, is it not the communion of the body of Christ?" (1 Corinthians 10:16.)

Was not the ordinance physical, as was the crucifixion? And as was the resurrection? There was nothing mystical about it. Neither were there to be repeated "sacrifices" as though He died many times on many altars in many congregations in the nations of the world. Said Paul to the Romans:

"Now if we be dead with Christ, we believe that we shall also live with him: knowing that Christ being raised from the dead dieth no more; death hath no more dominion over him. For in that he died, he died unto sin once: but in that he liveth, he liveth unto God." (Romans 6:8-10.)

He wrote to the Hebrews: "This man, after he had offered one sacrifice for sins for ever, sat down on the right hand of God.... For by one offering he hath perfected for ever them that are sanctified." (Hebrews 10:12, 14.)

Paul taught the importance of partaking of these emblems worthily. "Whosoever shall eat this bread, and drink this cup of the Lord, unworthily, shall be guilty of the body and blood of the Lord. But let a man examine himself, and so let him eat of that bread, and drink of that cup. For he that eateth and drinketh unworthily, eateth and drinketh damnation to himself, not discerning the Lord's body. For this cause many are weak and sickly among you, and many sleep." (1 Corinthians 11:27-30.)

The Corinthians were in the process of apostatizing from the faith, as is evidenced by their rejection of the entire doctrine of resurrection. Evidently some returned to idolatrous practices, including offering meat sacrifices to idols. Most vigorously Paul launched out against this. The Corinthians could not serve two masters. (Matthew 6:24.) They could not partake of the Lord's Supper and at the same time eat of food sacrificed to idols!

"What say I then? that the idol is any thing, or that which is offered in sacrifice to idols is any thing? But I say, that the things which the Gentiles sacrifice, they sacrifice to devils, and not to God: and I would not that ye should have fellowship with devils. Ye cannot drink the cup of the Lord, and the cup of devils: ye cannot be partakers of the Lord's table, and of the table of devils." (1 Corinthians 10:19-21.)

Did Paul know what James had written about consistency? "Out of the same mouth proceedeth blessing and cursing. My brethren, these things ought not so to be. Doth a fountain send forth at the same place sweet water and bitter? Can the fig tree, my brethren, bear olive berries? either a vine, figs? so can no fountain both yield salt water and fresh." (James 3:10-12.)

So Paul taught the sanctity of the sacrament of the Lord's Supper. It was all a great and holy reality to him and a testimony of:

1. The physical crucifixion of the physical Son of God.

2. Physical emblems—the bread and the cup—both to be taken separately in remembrance of the Savior's death.

3. The importance of partaking worthily.

Chapter Eight

THE HOLY GHOST

*T*HE THIRD MEMBER of the Godhead was of vital importance to Paul. This divine Being became a companion to him, gave him direction in his travels, and even participated in the call that came to him and his friend Barnabas. This call had great significance, not only for the assignment given these two men, but also because of the manner in which it came.

Luke records:

"Now there were in the church that was at Antioch certain prophets and teachers; as Barnabas, and Simeon that was called Niger, and Lucius of Cyrene, and Manaen, which had been brought up with Herod the tetrarch, and Saul.

"As they ministered to the Lord, and fasted, the Holy Ghost said, Separate me Barnabas and Saul for the work whereunto I have called them.

"And when they had fasted and prayed, and laid their hands on them, they sent them away.

"So they, being sent forth by the Holy Ghost, departed unto Seleucia; and from thence they sailed to Cyprus." (Acts 13:1-4.)

Here was a direct revelation to the prophets of the early church, coming with a specific purpose that was accomplished immediately. It addressed itself to the very heart of the manner by which men are chosen to enter God's ministry. They must be called by revelation!

Paul elaborated on this point in writing to the Hebrews when he said: "No man taketh this honour unto himself, but he that is called of God, as was Aaron." (Hebrews 5:4.)

And how was Aaron called? By revelation to a prophet! The Almighty said to his prophet Moses: "Take thou unto thee Aaron thy brother, and his sons with him, from among the children of Israel, that he may minister unto me in the priest's office, even Aaron, Nadab and Abihu, Eleazar and Ithamar, Aaron's sons." (Exodus 28:1.)

Evidently in this instance God spoke. In the case of Paul and Barnabas, it was the Holy Ghost who gave their revelation. But both are divine, both are members of the Godhead, the presiding authority in the universe. There is complete oneness of purpose among them. (John 17:11, 21.)

The Holy Ghost, therefore, was active in the ministry of the early church. Jesus had promised it. (John 14:26.) And note this:

"The former treatise have I made, O Theophilus, of all that Jesus began both to do and teach, until the day in which he was taken up, after that he through the Holy Ghost had given commandments unto the apostles whom he had chosen:

"To whom also he shewed himself alive after his passion by many infallible proofs, being seen of them forty days, and speaking of the things pertaining to the kingdom of God: and, being assembled together with them, commanded them that they should not depart from Jerusalem, but wait for the promise of the Father, which, saith he, ye have heard of me.

"For John truly baptized with water; but ye shall be baptized with the Holy Ghost not many days hence.

"When they therefore were come together, they asked of him, saying, Lord, wilt thou at this time restore again the kingdom to Israel?

"And he said unto them, It is not for you to know the times or the seasons, which the Father hath put in his own power. But ye shall receive power, after that the Holy Ghost is come upon you: and ye shall be witnesses unto me both in Jerusalem, and in all Judaea, and in Samaria, and unto the uttermost part of the earth.

"And when he had spoken these things, while they beheld, he was taken up; and a cloud received him out of their sight.

"And while they looked stedfastly toward heaven as he went up, behold, two men stood by them in white apparel; which also said, Ye men of Galilee, why stand ye gazing up into heaven? this same Jesus, which is taken up from you into heaven, shall so come in like manner as ye have seen him go into heaven.

"Then returned they unto Jerusalem from the mount called Olivet, which is from Jerusalem a sabbath day's journey." (Acts 1:1-12.)

What were some of the duties of this Spirit? He would be a revelator and a teacher, guaranteeing consistent divine guidance in the Lord's own church. The Lord said:

"I tell you the truth; It is expedient for you that I go away: for if I go not away, the Comforter will not come unto you; but if I depart, I will send him unto you.

"And when he is come, he will reprove the world of sin, and of righteousness, and of judgment: of sin, because they believe not on me; of righteousness, because I go to my Father, and ye see me no more; of judgment, because the prince of this world is judged.

"I have yet many things to say unto you, but ye cannot bear them now.

"Howbeit when he, the Spirit of truth, is come, he will guide you into all truth: for he shall not speak of himself; but whatsoever he shall hear, that shall he speak: and he will shew you things to come. He shall glorify me: for he shall receive of mine, and shall shew it unto you." (John 16:7-14.)

Paul wrote to the Corinthians, saying: "God hath revealed them unto us by his Spirit: for the Spirit searcheth all things, yea, the deep things of God. For what man knoweth the things of a man, save the spirit of man which is in him? even so the things of God knoweth no man, but the Spirit of God." (1 Corinthians 2:10-11.)

Baptism is required by the Christ. It includes baptism of fire and the Holy Ghost, as well as immersion in water. (Matthew 3:11.) The gift of the Holy Ghost was bestowed by

the laying on of the hands of those in authority, following
water baptism. That it must be done by proper authority is
evidenced in this episode:

"When the apostles which were at Jerusalem heard that Samaria had received the word of God, they sent unto them Peter and John: who, when they were come down, prayed for them, that they might receive the Holy Ghost: (for as yet he was fallen upon none of them: only they were baptized in the name of the Lord Jesus.) Then laid they their hands on them, and they received the Holy Ghost.

"And when Simon saw that through laying on of the apostles' hands the Holy Ghost was given, he offered them money, saying, Give me also this power, that on whomsoever I lay hands, he may receive the Holy Ghost.

"But Peter said unto him, Thy money perish with thee, because thou hast thought that the gift of God may be purchased with money." (Acts 8:14-20.)

The Holy Ghost guided Philip in his travels. (Acts 8:27-39.) The Spirit was central to the conversion of Cornelius. (Acts 10:44.) The Spirit sent Paul to Macedonia. (Acts 16:6-8.)

The direction given to Peter and the other apostles is shown in this: "We have sent therefore Judas and Silas, who shall also tell you the same things by mouth. For it seemed good to the Holy Ghost, and to us, to lay upon you no greater burden than these necessary things; that ye abstain from meats offered to idols, and from blood, and from things strangled, and from fornication: from which if ye keep yourselves, ye shall do well. Fare ye well." (Acts 15:27-29.)

The Holy Ghost made the brethren "overseers" to the Saints (Acts 20:28) and witnessed in "every city." (Acts 20:23.)

As Nicodemus was told so plainly, the Holy Ghost was given to the church to inspire and guide all its members as a part of complete baptism. The baptism of the Spirit was as much a part of the ordinance as was immersion in water. By our righteous living we qualify for the ministrations of the Spirit.

Paul asked, "What? know ye not that your body is the temple of the Holy Ghost which is in you, which ye have of God, and ye are not your own? For ye are bought with a price:

therefore glorify God in your body, and in your spirit, which are God's." (1 Corinthians 6:19-20.)

Stephen was filled with the Holy Ghost at the time of his martyrdom. (Acts 7:55.)

Speaking to the Thessalonians, Paul explained, "Our gospel came not unto you in word only, but also in power, and in the Holy Ghost, and in much assurance; as ye know what manner of men we were among you for your sake. And ye became followers of us, and of the Lord, having received the word in much affliction, with joy of the Holy Ghost." (1 Thessalonians 1:5-6.)

Paul's discussion of the gifts of the Spirit, one of several classic dissertations, is found in 1 Corinthians, chapters 12 and 14. Among other things he affirms that "no man speaking by the Spirit of God calleth Jesus accursed: and that no man can say that Jesus is the Lord, but by the Holy Ghost." (1 Corinthians 12:3.)

Both chapters merit careful and prayerful reading, as they provide further enlightenment on the workings of the Spirit.

So the members of the Godhead are three, and this Paul understood. They are Father, Son, and Holy Ghost. Each is divine, each is a Person. One in purpose and intent, each is fully harmonious in the direction of the work.

Chapter Nine

THE MEANING OF

BAPTISM

W HEN JOHN THE BAPTIST began his own ministry, he preached of the forthcoming ministry of the Savior and taught the doctrine of baptism in water for the remission of sins. But water baptism was not enough. There must follow the baptism of fire and the Holy Ghost, coming through Christ, for whom John prepared the way. (Matthew 3:11.)

Is water baptism necessary? Jesus taught this principle and set the pattern by being baptized himself, "for thus it becometh us to fulfill all righteousness." (Matthew 3:13-15.)

Is it a command for all? It is for all who understand the gospel and repent of their sins. Jesus commanded: "Go ye therefore, and teach all nations, baptizing them in the name of the Father, and of the Son, and of the Holy Ghost: teaching them to observe all things whatsoever I have commanded you: and, lo, I am with you alway, even unto the end of the world." (Matthew 28:19-20.)

Or, as quoted by Mark: "He said unto them, Go ye into all the world, and preach the gospel to every creature. He that believeth and is baptized shall be saved; but he that believeth not shall be damned." (Mark 16:15-16.)

Note this important passage: "All the people that heard

37

him, and the publicans, justified God, being baptized with the baptism of John. But the Pharisees and lawyers rejected the counsel of God against themselves, being not baptized of him." (Luke 7:29-30.)

There are four purposes in water baptism:

1. To enter the church.
2. To receive a remission of sins.
3. To commemorate the burial and resurrection of Christ.
4. To open the way to receive the gift of the Holy Ghost.

What did Paul teach about baptism?

First, he submitted to it himself, as did Christ. When he was approached by Ananias and came to understand the facts about Jesus and His gospel, Paul was given the ordinance and thereby received a remision of his sins. Said Ananias to him:

"The God of our fathers hath chosen thee, that thou shouldest know his will, and see that Just One, and shouldest hear the voice of his mouth. For thou shalt be his witness unto all men of what thou hast seen and heard. And now why tarriest thou? arise, and be baptized, and wash away thy sins, calling on the name of the Lord." (Acts 22:14-16.)

Not only did Paul accept baptism for himself, but he also required this ordinance of his converts. We have a clear illustration in his dealings with the jailor, who "called for a light, and sprang in, and came trembling, and fell down before Paul and Silas, and brought them out, and said, Sirs, what must I do to be saved?

"And they said, Believe on the Lord Jesus Christ, and thou shalt be saved, and thy house.

"And they spake unto him the word of the Lord, and to all that were in his house.

"And he took them the same hour of the night, and washed their stripes; and was baptized, he and all his, straightway. And when he had brought them into his house, he set meat before them, and rejoiced, believing in God with all his house." (Acts 16:29-34.)

Peter already had taught baptism:

"Now when they heard this, they were pricked in their

heart, and said unto Peter and to the rest of the apostles, Men and brethren, what shall we do?

"Then Peter said unto them, Repent, and be baptized every one of you in the name of Jesus Christ for the remission of sins, and ye shall receive the gift of the Holy Ghost. For the promise is unto you, and to your children, and to all that are afar off, even as many as the Lord our God shall call.

"And with many other words did he testify and exhort, saying, Save yourselves from this untoward generation." (Acts 2:37-40.)

Now Paul followed the pattern. From him we have this important episode:

"It came to pass, that, while Apollos was at Corinth, Paul having passed through the upper coasts came to Ephesus: and finding certain disciples, he said unto them, Have ye received the Holy Ghost since ye believed? And they said unto him, We have not so much as heard whether there be any Holy Ghost.

"And he said unto them, Unto what then were ye baptized? And they said, Unto John's baptism.

"Then said Paul, John verily baptized with the baptism of repentance, saying unto the people, that they should believe on him which should come after him, that is, on Christ Jesus.

"When they heard this, they were baptized in the name of the Lord Jesus.

"And when Paul had laid his hands upon them, the Holy Ghost came on them; and they spake with tongues, and prophesied." (Acts 19:1-6.)

Here it is noted that Paul acted according to the established order of the church:

1. He made certain of the conversion of the group.

2. He baptized them.

3. He laid his hands upon them for the reception of the Holy Ghost.

What is the importance of this form of baptism? Why is immersion the only acceptable way?

As the sacrament of the Lord's Supper commemorates the atonement on the cross, so immersion baptism commemorates the Lord's burial and resurrection. As Christ was buried in the tomb, so we are buried in the waters of baptism. As He came forth from the tomb to a newness of life in resurrection, so we come forth from immersion in water to a newness of life in the gospel. Paul explained to the Romans:

"Know ye not, that so many of us as were baptized into Jesus Christ were baptized into his death? Therefore we are buried with him by baptism into death: that like as Christ was raised up from the dead by the glory of the Father, even so we also should walk in newness of life. For if we have been planted together in the likeness of his death, we shall be also in the likeness of his resurrection." (Romans 6:3-5.)

He taught the Colossians the identical doctrine: "Buried with him in baptism, wherein also ye are risen with him through the faith of the operation of God, who hath raised him from the dead." (Colossians 2:12.)

Baptism is not for infants. Some teach that babies are to be freed from the original sin by baptism, although this is not the doctrine of Christ. The original sin brought death into the world, and death is overcome by the Lord's resurrection, for thereby all will be raised from the tomb. Paul made his teachings abundantly clear to the Corinthians. (1 Corinthians 15.)

Who should be baptized? Those who can be taught (Matthew 28:19; Mark 16:15-16) and those who believe and repent (Acts 2:37-39). Baptism is for the remission of our personal sins and is granted to those who have faith and repent.

John the Baptist, the Savior, and the apostles all taught the same doctrine:

1. Baptism is required.

2. Through baptism we gain a remission of our personal sins.

3. By baptism we gain admission to the church.

Did not Jesus explain the essential nature of this ordinance to Nicodemus? (John 3:3-5.) To say that baptism is not necessary is to deny one of the basic doctrines of Christ.

But who may perform this ordinance? From the days of Moses the scriptures teach that the ordinances of the Lord could be performed only by men specially chosen for this priestly office. For this reason Aaron and his sons were given divine appointment. (Exodus 28:1.) Paul taught that all ministers for Christ must be called "as was Aaron." (Hebrews 5:4.)

Such selection requires revelation to a living prophet, so prophets were placed in the Christian church and were to remain there "for the work of the ministry." (Ephesians 4:11-14.)

Chapter Ten

THE STRUCTURE OF THE CHURCH

*P*AUL GIVES US the greatest detail in the scriptures concerning the organization of the original church of Jesus Christ. The Savior Himself installed apostles and seventies (Luke 6:14; 10:1), although other officers are not listed in the four Gospels. They came later. But a church there most definitely was! (Matthew 16:18; 18:17; Acts 2:46-47; 11:22; 15:22; 20:17; 20:28; 1 Corinthians 15:9; Ephesians 1:22; 1 Timothy 5:16; James 5:14; 3 John 1:10.)

As Paul described its organization, he emphasized: "Ye are no more strangers and foreigners, but fellowcitizens with the saints, and of the household of God; and are built upon the foundation of the apostles and prophets, Jesus Christ himself being the chief corner stone; in whom all the building fitly framed together groweth unto an holy temple in the Lord: in whom ye also are builded together for an habitation of God through the Spirit." (Ephesians 2:19-22.)

This is a vital point. The church was founded upon Christ and the apostles and prophets!

42   Paul went further in the fourth chapter of Ephesians when he said that the Lord "gave some, apostles; and some, prophets; and some, evangelists; and some, pastors and

teachers." (Ephesians 4:11.) Then he explained their functions:

"For the perfecting of the saints, for the work of the
ministry, for the edifying of the body of Christ: till we all come
in the unity of the faith, and of the knowledge of the Son of
God, unto a perfect man, unto the measure of the stature of
the fulness of Christ: that we henceforth be no more children,
tossed to and fro, and carried about with every wind of doctrine, by the slight of men, and cunning craftiness, whereby
they lie in wait to deceive; but speaking the truth in love, may
grow up into him in all things, which is the head, even Christ:
from whom the whole body fitly joined together and compacted by that which every joint supplieth, according to the
effectual working in the measure of every part, maketh in-
crease of the body unto the edifying of itself in love." (Ephesians 4:12-16.)

Let us list these functions:

1. For the perfecting of the Saints. This recalls the
Savior's instruction: "Be ye ... perfect, even as your Father
which is in heaven is perfect." (Matthew 5:48.) Paul explains
the expected perfection further in saying that we are to attain
"unto a perfect man, unto the measure of the stature of the
fulness of Christ."

2. In that connection he continues saying that these
church officers are for the edifying of the members. How
could the Saints perfect themselves without inspired instruction?

3. For the work of the ministry. The book of Acts and all
the epistles endorse this fact. Who carried on the work? The
answer is obvious.

This "work of the ministry" necessarily included calling
other men to positions in the church as they were needed.
Hence, there were "evangelists; and ... pastors and teachers"
for the work of the ministry and the perfecting of the Saints.

One outstanding case in point is the call to Paul and
Barnabas, issued by the Holy Ghost but directed to whom?
The apostles assembled in Antioch! This event recalls the
words of Amos: "Surely the Lord God will do nothing, but he

revealeth his secret unto his servants the prophets." (Amos 3:7.) It surely applies to the "work of the ministry."

4. These officers were to remain in the church "till we all come in the unity of the faith, and of the knowledge of the Son of God, unto a perfect man, unto the measure of the stature of the fulness of Christ."

5. They were installed to protect the members from false doctrine: "That we henceforth be no more children, tossed to and fro, and carried about with every wind of doctrine, by the sleight of men, and cunning craftiness, whereby they lie in wait to deceive; but speaking the truth in love, may grow up into him in all things, which is the head, even Christ."

6. Their duty was to preserve unity in the faith, and they were to remain in the church to lead and edify the members until that unity is achieved.

The oneness of the church was greatly emphasized by Paul. In this same epistle he stressed: "There is one body, and one Spirit, even as ye are called in one hope of your calling; one Lord, one faith, one baptism, one God and Father of all, who is above all, and through all, and in you all. But unto every one of us is given grace according to the measure of the gift of Christ." (Ephesians 4:4-7.)

To the Romans he said: "As we have many members in one body, and all members have not the same office: so we, being many, are one body in Christ, and every one members one of another." (Romans 12:4-5.)

Could Paul have been more emphatic than when he declared that the whole body should be fitly joined together? He wrote to the Corinthians in these same terms:

"As the body is one, and hath many members, and all the members of that one body, being many, are one body: so also is Christ. For by one Spirit are we all baptized into one body, whether we be Jews or Gentiles, whether we be bond or free; and have been all made to drink into one Spirit. For the body is not one member, but many.

"If the foot shall say, Because I am not the hand, I am not of the body; is it therefore not of the body? And if the ear shall say, Because I am not the eye, I am not of the body; is it there-

fore not of the body? If the whole body were an eye, where
were the hearing? If the whole were hearing, where were the
smelling?

"But now hath God set the members every one of them in the body, as it hath pleased him. And if they were all one member, where were the body? But now are they many members, yet but one body. And the eye cannot say unto the hand, I have no need of thee: nor again the head to the feet, I have no need of you.

"Nay, much more those members of the body, which seem to be more feeble, are necessary." (1 Corinthians 12: 12-22.)

Paul particularly emphasized "that there should be no schism in the body; but that the members should have the same care one for another." (1 Corinthians 12:25.) He again stressed:

"God hath set some in the church, first apostles, secondarily prophets, thirdly teachers, after that miracles, then gifts of healings, helps, government, diversities of tongues. Are all apostles? are all prophets? are all teachers? are all workers of miracles? Have all the gifts of healing? do all speak with tongues? do all interpret?" (1 Corinthians 12:28-30.)

It was complete oneness and unity among the Saints for which Jesus had prayed. (John 17:11.)

No division exists in Christ. Divisions are departures from Christ. The protection provided for the members in this regard rests with apostles, prophets, evangelists, pastors, and teachers. Then must not these officers be preserved in the church? Should they not continue to function until we reach the perfection of which Paul speaks? If the foundation of any structure is removed, what befalls the structure?

As the church grew in its beginning years, other officers were added, such as these pastors and teachers of whom Paul spoke. Elders were ordained in every branch of the church. (Acts 14:23; 15:6; 1 Timothy 5:17.) Bishops and priests were named. (1 Timothy 3:1; Titus 1:7; Philippians 1:1.) Deacons were chosen. (1 Timothy 3:10; Philippians 1:1.) Evangelists are mentioned in 2 Timothy 4:5, and high priests are spoken of in Hebrews 5.

So the structure of the church included:
    Apostles
    Prophets
    High priests
    Seventies
    Elders
    Evangelists
    Bishops (who were pastors)
    Priests
    Teachers
    Deacons

They were to work as one—jointly fit and compacted together. To use Paul's comparison, "the eye cannot say unto the hand, I have no need of thee." And, of course, the bishop or priest was never authorized to say to either apostle or prophet, "I have no need of thee."

But where are these officers today—the foundations of the church?

Can the true church exist without them?

The true church of Christ has many clear marks of identification, and its structural organization is one of the most important. No building can stand without its foundation.

Chapter Eleven

THE FALLING AWAY

*P*AUL LIVED to see the structure that he had helped to build corrode, deteriorate, and fall apart. In Christian times the first sign of apostasy appeared in the early days of the Lord's own ministry. His pure doctrine was in such contrast to the false teachings to which the people of that day were accustomed that it frightened away his followers. We read in the sixth chapter of John:

"Many . . . of his disciples, when they had heard this, said, This is an hard saying; who can hear it? When Jesus knew in himself that his disciples murmured at it, he said unto them, Doth this offend you? What and if ye shall see the Son of man ascend up where he was before?" (John 6:60-62.)

And then comes this sad note: "From that time many of his disciples went back, and walked no more with him. Then said Jesus unto the twelve, Will ye also go away? Then Simon Peter answered him, Lord, to whom shall we go? thou hast the words of eternal life. And we believe and are sure that thou art that Christ, the Son of the living God." (John 6:66-69.)

On the day of Pentecost, following the Lord's Passion, only 120 of His followers attended their meeting.

"These all continued with one accord in prayer and supplication, with the women, and Mary the mother of Jesus, and with his brethren.

"And in those days Peter stood up in the midst of the disciples, and said, (the number of names together were about an hundred and twenty,) Men and brethren, this scripture must needs have been fulfilled, which the Holy Ghost by the mouth of David spake before concerning Judas, which was guide to them that took Jesus.

"For he was numbered with us, and had obtained part of this ministry." (Acts 1:14-17.)

Here Peter spoke of the need for a successor to Judas, "and the lot fell upon Matthias." (Acts 1:26.)

Conversions soon added thousands to the church, and the work was taken even to the Gentiles. But soon both sin and false teachers arose, causing many to fall away.

Paul was powerful in his defense of the gospel, but apostasy continued. He had established the church at Corinth with high hopes for it, but now came both dissension and false teachers denying Christ and the resurrection. He wrote to his converts there, saying:

"I beseech you, brethren, by the name of our Lord Jesus Christ, that ye all speak the same thing, and that there be no divisions among you; but that ye be perfectly joined together in the same mind and in the same judgment.

"For it hath been declared unto me of you, my brethren, by them which are of the house of Chloe, that there are contentions among you.

"Now this I say, that every one of you saith, I am of Paul; and I of Apollos: and I of Cephas; and I of Christ.

"Is Christ divided? was Paul crucified for you? or were ye baptized in the name of Paul?" (1 Corinthians 1:10-13.)

Paul's discourse defending the resurrection is a masterpiece, a testimony of the resurrection of Christ that will stand for all time:

"Now is Christ risen from the dead, and become the firstfruits of them that slept. For since by man came death, by man came also the resurrection of the dead. For as in Adam all die, even so in Christ shall all be made alive. But every man in his own order: Christ the firstfruits; afterward they that are Christ's at his coming." (1 Corinthians 15:20-23.)

To the Galatians he said: "I marvel that ye are so soon removed from him that called you into the grace of Christ unto another gospel: which is not another; but there be some that trouble you, and would pervert the gospel of Christ. But though we, or an angel from heaven, preach any other gospel unto you than that which we have preached unto you, let him be accursed." (Galatians 1:6-8.)

He told the Thessalonians that "the mystery of iniquity doth already work." (2 Thessalonians 2:7.)

He warned Titus of the influx of deceivers: "They profess that they know God; but in works they deny him, being abominable, and disobedient, and unto every good work reprobate." (Titus 1:10-11, 16.)

To Timothy he wrote this sad prediction: "In the last days perilous times shall come. For men shall be lovers of their own selves, covetous, boasters, proud, blasphemers, disobedient to parents, unthankful, unholy, without natural affection, trucebreakers, false accusers, incontinent, fierce, despisers of those that are good, traitors, heady, highminded, lovers of pleasures more than lovers of God; having a form of godliness; but denying the power thereof: from such turn away.

"For of this sort are they which creep into houses, and lead captive silly women laden with sins, led away with divers lusts, ever learning, and never able to come to the knowledge of the truth."(2 Timothy 3:1-7.)

Peter joined him in his warnings, saying:

"There were false prophets . . . among the people, even as there shall be false teachers among you, who privily shall bring in damnable heresies, even denying the Lord that bought them, and bring upon themselves swift destruction.

"And many shall follow their pernicious ways; by reason of whom the way of truth shall be evil spoken of.

"And through covetousness shall they with feigned words make merchandise of you: whose judgment now of a long time lingereth not, and their damnation slumbereth not." (2 Peter 2:1-3.)

Jude did likewise: "Beloved, remember ye the words which were spoken before of the apostles of our Lord Jesus Christ; how that they told you there should be mockers in the last time, who should walk after their own ungodly lusts.

These be they who separate themselves, sensual, having not the Spirit." (Jude 1:17-19.)

There was a widespread belief among the Saints that Christ's second coming would occur in the day in which they then lived. Combatting this false idea, the brethren pointed to the impending apostasy. Said Paul in writing to the Thessalonians:

"We beseech you, brethren, by the coming of our Lord Jesus Christ, and by our gathering together unto him, that ye be not soon shaken in mind, or be troubled, neither by spirit, nor by word, nor by letter as from us, as that the day of Christ is at hand.

"Let no man deceive you by any means: for that day shall not come, except there come a falling away first, and that man of sin be revealed, the son of perdition; who opposeth and exalteth himself above all that is called God, or that is worshipped; so that he as God sitteth in the temple of God, shewing himself that he is God." (2 Thessalonians 2:1-4.)

A Roman Catholic translation of the Bible (New American, 1972) gives this rendering of Paul's letter: "We beg you brothers, not to be so easily agitated or terrified . . . into believing that the day of Christ is here. Let no one seduce you . . . since the *mass apostasy* has not yet occurred." (2 Thessalonians 2:2-3.) To this is attached a footnote: "They should not allow themselves to be duped into this way of thinking, for a religious apostasy is destined to precede the Lord's Second Coming."

Another Catholic version (Knox) reads: "Do not let anyone lead you astray. The apostasy must come first."

So Paul saw apostasy coming and fought against it, but he could not stay the tide. He did give his all in the effort, however, and he died a martyr to the cause.

Chapter Twelve

FAITH AND WORKS

*P*AUL IS QUOTED or misquoted many times as some attempt to justify the doctrine of salvation by grace alone, and "not of works, lest any man should boast." Paul's actual words are: "By grace are ye saved through faith; and that not of yourselves: it is the gift of God: not of works, lest any man should boast." (Ephesians 2:8-9.)

No one understanding the facts would deny that we are saved by the grace and mercy of God. Only He could open the door to our salvation. He did so out of His infinite grace, and in mercy He invites us to enter. But He laid down certain requirements by which we first must qualify to receive His blessing.

Salvation is not a matter of going to heaven to enjoy a blissful existence of ease and entertainment for all eternity. It is not a matter of being given front-row seats to see the marvels of heaven unfold. Since we are the children of God (Acts 17:28-29), there is a purpose in our existence, and that purpose is to grow and develop, eventually to become like our Father in heaven. (Matthew 5:48.)

Did not Jesus command us to become perfect like God? What did He mean? He meant exactly what He said: Develop Christlike traits of character! Become like Him!

Salvation is not a gift to be bestowed upon us for the ask-

51

ing any more than is a college degree. To obtain a medical doctorate, for example, requires study, practice, developing skills, and obtaining knowledge until in our college work we have grown to that stage of perfection in medicine that justifies certification and bestowal of the degree.

Which is easier, to become a good doctor or to become perfect like God? Neither is accomplished easily.

Developing all the facets of perfection like unto God also requires growth, development, study, and practice. This is what salvation means. Many will not be saved but will be condemned on Judgment Day. And why? Because they did not qualify. (Matthew 25.) We are told that on Judgment Day we will be judged according to our acts in the flesh. If our works qualify us for salvation we shall be saved, but if they do not we shall be damned.

Part of the qualification is mentioned by the Lord in this scripture: "He that believeth and is baptized shall be saved; but he that believeth not shall be damned." (Mark 16:16.)

If we are to become perfect like God, pause and think for a moment what an eternity of study, discipline, growth, and development will be required. Let us not misunderstand salvation and suppose that it is like receiving a free ticket for admission to heaven. Our destiny is not to sit in some holy grandstand. It is to inherit the things of God and be glorified together with the Lord Jesus Christ. Note that word *together*. Paul explained our great potential. Said he:

"The Spirit itself beareth witness with our spirit, that we are the children of God: and if children, then heirs; heirs of God, and joint-heirs with Christ; if so be that we suffer with him, that we may be also glorified together." (Romans 8:16-17.)

Paul also makes it clear that we will be required to develop perfect traits of character to qualify us for such a high estate. They must reach the fulness of the measure of Christ's perfection. (Ephesians 4:13.)

Through His grace He gives us His gospel plan as an opportunity to achieve, but we must grow into this opportunity. Compare our present state with Christ's perfection. Have we not much growth to develop? His grace gives us the opportunity to become like Him, but our works must provide the development and growth to achieve this potential. He opens the door, but we must take the steps to enter. He will not push us in.

Strictly out of His grace He died for us, but unless we qualify for His blessing by our good works, we still may be damned. (Matthew 25; Mark 16:16.)

If He had not died for us there would be no salvation. But He allowed Himself to be crucified, and so salvation came by His grace. The free gift of His life through His grace made it possible, but we still must obey Him to qualify to receive His blessing.

One teacher gave the following as a simple illustration: We need a "ladder" by which to ascend to His presence. As a free gift, God provides the ladder, which is His gospel. But we must climb that ladder step by step by our own effort. He will not climb it for us, nor will He lift us to the top without effort on our part. We are saved by the ladder, which is given by His grace. We could not provide the ladder ourselves, for it is beyond our power. Therefore, as Paul says, salvation is not of ourselves, lest anyone should boast, but is a gift of God. We could not boast over the possession of that ladder, for we had nothing to do with providing it. The ladder came to us by grace as a favor—freely given—from God.

An important passage on this subject is also given us by Paul: "We are his workmanship, created in Christ Jesus unto good works, which God hath before ordained that we should walk in them." (Ephesians 2:10.)

Note that in Christ we are created *to do His work!* We were ordained of God to walk in "good works." To say that no works at all are needed on our part is to defy and deny the facts. Why did Paul bring up the matter of works?

One reason was that the law of Moses had been fulfilled in Christ; the works of the law were obsolete and no longer valid. It should be remembered that Paul was in the midst of a conflict between Jews who were loyal to the law of Moses and those who properly understood the new covenant introduced by Christ.

It was truly a new covenant and a clear departure from

the law of Moses, a whole new system of salvation introduced by Jesus, who fulfilled the law of Moses and gave us the gospel instead. The law of Moses was a system of performances—of works, we may say. It was a schoolmaster to bring people up to the point where they could live the gospel. (Galatians 3:24-27.)

Paul spoke of these works as having become "dead works" with the coming of Christ. (Hebrews 6:1; 9:14.) And why were they dead? Because they no longer applied, being supplanted by Christ's gospel. They were set aside. The new had replaced the old.

Hence, under the gospel, the law of Moses with all its numerous works was now powerless to save.

Many Jewish converts wanted to merge the law and the gospel. Remember Paul's dispute with Peter over this very subject. Many refused to give up the law of Moses. They were converted to Christ but did not understand that a new covenant had come that fulfilled and cancelled the old law.

Should circumcision be carried over into the gospel, for example?

Paul said no, while others said yes. But why should anyone insist that Gentile converts bow to an ancient Jewish requirement that was not even a part of Christ's gospel? They came from an entirely different environment. Must they now bow to outmoded Jewish customs that were completely foreign to them?

Circumcision was Jewish. These converts were Gentiles, Paul argued, and to bring circumcision into the gospel would be to mix the two. It would be like putting new wine into old bottles, which would burst.

So what was the decision? No circumcision was required! There would be no mixing of the dead works of the law with the saving works of the gospel of Christ!

How glad the Saints in Antioch must have been when it "pleased . . . the apostles and elders, with the whole church, to send chosen men of their own company to Antioch with Paul and Barnabas; namely Judas surnamed Barsabas, and Silas, chief men among the brethren:

"And they wrote letters by them after this manner; The apostles and elders and brethren send greeting unto the brethren which are of the Gentiles in Antioch and Syria and Cilicia:

"Forasmuch as we have heard, that certain which went out from us have troubled you with words, subverting your souls, saying, Ye must be circumcised, and keep the law: *to whom we gave no such commandment:*

"It seemed good unto us, being assembled with one accord, to send chosen men unto you with our beloved Barnabas and Paul, men that have hazarded their lives for the name of our Lord Jesus Christ.

"We have sent therefore Judas and Silas, who shall also tell you the same things by mouth.

"For it seemed good to the Holy Ghost, and to us, to lay upon you no greater burden than these necessary things; that ye abstain from meats offered to idols, and from blood, and from things strangled, and from fornication: from which if ye keep yourselves, ye shall do well. Fare ye well." (Acts 15: 22-29. Italics added.)

And how glad were the Galatians to receive this message: "Knowing that a man is not justified by the works of the law, but by the faith of Jesus Christ, even we have believed in Jesus Christ, that we might be justified by the faith of Christ, and not by the works of the law: for by the works of the law shall no flesh be justified." (Galatians 2:16.)

Thus the air was cleared. The dead works of the law were no longer required. It was with such a background that Paul could write, "Not of works, lest any man should boast," including the dead works of the law. (Ephesians 2:9.)

He preached a gospel of both faith and works—Christian works. Not Mosaic, but Christian! And he had good reason to do so, for Christ had set the pattern before him.

Christian works? "Believe on the Lord Jesus Christ, and thou shalt be saved"? (Acts 16:31.) Of course!

But belief in Christ required *obedience to Christ,* and that meant works—His kind. And what were they? They were many.

First came faith and repentance, followed by baptism, for this ordinance was no more to be eliminated than was repentance. Can anyone enter the presence of God while still in his sins? Is there any other means of being cleansed before Him? Certainly not! The Almighty Himself instituted baptism for this very purpose—the remission of sins.

Baptism is the gateway to His presence. Who has the right to abolish it? Are not the words of the Lord to Nicodemus sufficient? Nicodemus was told that he could not even see the kingdom of God without baptism, and neither can we. (John 3:1-5.) Baptism is part of the works of the gospel and cannot be discarded. Neither can other requirements.

When Paul stated that works alone could not save us, he was perfectly correct, even regarding gospel works. For example, if we had no faith and no repentance but were baptized, could baptism itself save us? Certainly not. Faith and the other works of Christ are required also.

What did the Savior say about works? "The works that I do shall [ye] do also." (John 14:12.) He also said: "But I have greater witness than that of John: for the works which the Father hath given me to finish, the same works that I do, bear witness of me, that the Father hath sent me." (John 5:36.)

This quotation is interesting: "Then said they unto him, What shall we do, that we might work the works of God? Jesus answered and said unto them, This is the work of God, that ye believe on him whom he hath sent." (John 6:28-29.)

And this, of course, would require them to do His works. Faith without works is dead. (James 2:26.)

What are some of the other works of the gospel? Read the Sermon on the Mount for an answer. It is full of examples. And study the story of the Good Samaritan. What of the parable of the sower? Does it involve works? What of the twenty-fifth chapter of Matthew? Who can escape its impressive lesson?

Note a few more examples:

"Let your light so shine before men, that they may see your good works." (Matthew 5:16.) Our faith is only as strong as our obedience.

In the book of John we read of Jesus healing a blind man. "And his disciples asked him, saying, Master, who did sin, this man, or his parents, that he was born blind? Jesus answered, Neither hath this man sinned, nor his parents: but that the works of God should be made manifest in him. I must work the works of him that sent me, while it is day: the night cometh, when no man can work." (John 9:2-4.)

This also is meaningful: "Verily, verily, I say unto you, He that believeth on me, the works that I do shall he do also; and greater works than these shall he do; because I go unto my Father." (John 14:12.)

The Holy Ghost issued the call to Paul and Barnabas that they might do "the *work* whereunto I have called them." (Acts 13:2. Italics added.)

Paul urged the Corinthians: "Therefore, my beloved brethren, be ye stedfast, unmoveable, always abounding in the work of the Lord, forasmuch as ye know that your labour is not in vain in the Lord." (1 Corinthians 15:58.)

How often have we been told that on Judgment Day we will be judged according to our works in the flesh?

One of the most direct discussions on faith and works is this well-known passage from James:

"What doth it profit, my brethren, though a man say he hath faith, and have not works? can faith save him?

"If a brother or sister be naked, and destitute of daily food, and one of you say unto them, Depart in peace, be ye warmed and filled; nowithstanding ye give them not those things which are needful to the body; what doth it profit?

"Even so faith, if it hath not works, is dead, being alone.

"Yea, a man may say, Thou hast faith, and I have works: shew me thy faith without thy works, and I will shew thee my faith by my works. Thou believest that there is one God; thou doest well: the devils also believe, and tremble. But wilt thou know, O vain man, that faith without works is dead?

"Was not Abraham our father justified by works, when he had offered Isaac his son upon the altar? Seest thou how faith wrought with his works, and by works was faith made perfect?

"And the scripture was fulfilled which saith, Abraham

believed God, and it was imputed unto him for righteousness: and he was called the Friend of God. Ye see then how that by works a man is justified, and not by faith only.

"Likewise also was not Rahab the harlot justified by works, when she had received the messengers, and had sent them out another way?

"For as the body without the spirit is dead, so faith without works is dead also." (James 2:14-26.)

It was James also who said:

"But be ye doers of the word, and not hearers only, deceiving your own selves. For if any be a hearer of the word, and not a doer, he is like unto a man beholding his natural face in a glass: For he beholdeth himself, and goeth his way, and straightway forgetteth what manner of man he was.

"But whoso looketh into the perfect law of liberty, and continueth therein, he being not a forgetful hearer, but a doer of the work, this man shall be blessed in his deed." (James 1:22-25.)

Chapter Thirteen

RIGHTEOUS LIVING

*P*AUL TAUGHT VIGOROUSLY that the Saints must live the clean life, set proper examples of righteousness, and have an eye single to the work and glory of God. He lived in a day of great wickedness, when the idolatrous Gentiles whom he sought to convert were encouraged in immorality, even by their pagan religions.

This was especially true in Ephesus, where he opposed the sex cult of Diana of the Ephesians, and in Corinth. It was the case to a large extent with Athens, and with Rome, the seat of government, which was also a center of culture and sin.

Many of the Gentile Saints came out of just such an environment and had to learn by strict teaching that the Christian life is one of virtue. Chastity must be enthroned, for cleanliness of body, mind, and spirit are part and parcel of the way of life under the new and everlasting covenant.

This gave rise to Paul's message to the Corinthians, informing them that the Spirit of God must be allowed to dwell in them, and for this reason they must regard their bodies as temples of that Spirit, keeping them pure.

Family life entered into some of his covenants as well. Thus he wrote: "The body is not for fornication, but for the Lord; and the Lord for the body."

Then in his usual straightforward manner he continued: "Know ye not that your bodies are the members of

Christ? shall I then take the members of Christ, and make them the members of an harlot? God forbid.

"What? know ye not that he which is joined to an harlot is one body? for two, saith he, shall be one flesh. But he that is joined unto the Lord is one spirit.

60

"Flee fornication. Every sin that a man doeth is without the body; but he that committeth fornication sinneth against his own body.

"What? know ye not that your body is the temple of the Holy Ghost which is in you, which ye have of God, and ye are not your own? For ye are bought with a price: therefore glorify God in your body, and in your spirit, which are God's." (1 Corinthians 6:13-20.)

Paul broadened his subject also to cover other evils: "Know ye not that the unrighteous shall not inherit the kingdom of God? Be not deceived: neither fornicators, nor idolaters, nor adulterers, nor effeminate, nor abusers of themselves with mankind, nor thieves, nor covetous, nor drunkards, nor revilers, nor extortioners, shall inherit the kingdom of God." (1 Corinthians 6:9-10.)

Considering the conditions of the day and the customs that prevailed in those lands, we can more readily understand some of Paul's observations on family life. He said: "Now concerning the things whereof ye wrote unto me: It is good for a man not to touch a woman. Nevertheless, to avoid fornication, let every man have his own wife, and let every woman have her own husband." (1 Corinthians 7:1-2.)

Could this have given rise to other such comments? Note this:

"Now concerning virgins I have no commandment of the Lord: yet I give my judgment, as one that hath obtained mercy of the Lord to be faithful. I suppose therefore that this is good for the present distress, I say, that it is good for a man so to be.

"Art thou bound unto a wife? seek not to be loosed. Art thou loosed from a wife? seek not a wife.

"But and if thou marry, thou hast not sinned; and if a virgin marry, she hath not sinned. Nevertheless such shall have trouble in the flesh: but I spare you." (1 Corinthians 7:25-28.)

He also said:

"I say . . . to the unmarried and widows, It is good for them if they abide even as I. But if they cannot contain, let them marry: for it is better to marry than to burn.

"And unto the married I command, yet not I, but the Lord, Let not the wife depart from her husband: but and if she depart, let her remain unmarried, or be reconciled to her husband: and let not the husband put away his wife.

"But to the rest speak I, not the Lord: If any brother hath a wife that believeth not, and she be pleased to dwell with him, let him not put her away. And the woman which hath an husband that believeth not, and if he be pleased to dwell with her, let her not leave him. For the unbelieving husband is sanctified by the wife, and the unbelieving wife is sanctified by the husband: else were your children unclean; but now are they holy.

"But if the unbelieving depart, let him depart. A brother or a sister is not under bondage in such cases: but God hath called us to peace." (1 Corinthians 7:8-15.)

Paul knew that in part-member families nonmember spouses might be converted, as is the case today. So he wrote: "For what knowest thou, O wife, whether thou shalt save thy husband? or how knowest thou, O man, whether thou shalt save thy wife?" (1 Corinthians 7:16.)

Understanding the gospel as he did, Paul sensed fully the importance of marriage and the purpose of God in creating male and female. So it was that he declared: "Neither is the man without the woman, neither the woman without the man, in the Lord." (1 Corinthians 11:11.)

And isn't it comforting that he also said, "The woman is the glory of the man." (1 Corinthians 11:7.) Every man could well remember this statement.

We are not bound by Roman law nor by Grecian customs, so we need not be disturbed by some of Paul's seemingly unorthodox expressions. Whether men or women wore long or short hair was a matter of the custom of the day, without scriptural basis. And was it not merely a custom of the times that women could not speak in church, having nothing to do with gospel doctrine then any more than now?

Certainly Paul taught family life and harmony in the home. He required marriage for holders of the priesthood: "A bishop . . . must be blameless, the husband of one wife, vigilant, sober, of good behaviour, given to hospitality, apt to teach. . . . Likewise must the deacons be grave, not double-tongued, not given to much wine, not greedy of filthy lucre." (1 Timothy 3:2, 8.)

He instructed the husbands to rule well their own homes; otherwise, how could they govern the church? But they must rule only "in righteousness."

When he urged parents to have their children in subjection, wasn't he really talking about proper child training in the home? (1 Timothy 3:4-5.)

He certainly instructed fathers that they must not provoke their children to wrath (Ephesians 6:4), and he taught children to honor their parents: "Children, obey your parents in the Lord: for this is right. Honour thy father and mother; (which is the first commandment with promise;) that it may be well with thee, and thou mayest live long on the earth." (Ephesians 6:1-3.)

He spoke similarly to the Colossians:

"Whatsoever ye do in word or deed, do all in the name of the Lord Jesus, giving thanks to God and the Father by him.

"Wives, submit yourselves unto your own husbands, as it is fit in the Lord. Husbands, love your wives, and be not bitter against them. Children, obey your parents in all things: for this is well pleasing unto the Lord. Fathers, provoke not your children to anger, lest they be discouraged. Servants, obey in all things your masters according to the flesh; not with eye-service, as menpleasers; but in singleness of heart, fearing God: and whatsoever ye do, do it heartily, as to the Lord, and not unto men; knowing that of the Lord ye shall receive the reward of the inheritance: for ye serve the Lord Christ.

"But he that doeth wrong shall receive for the wrong which he hath done: and there is no respect of persons." (Colossians 3:17-25.)

Were there quarrels among the Saints? To meet any such problem, Paul wrote:

"Be renewed in the spirit of your mind; and . . . put on Righteous the new man, which after God is created in righteousness and *Living* true holiness.

"Wherefore putting away lying, speak every man truth with his neighbour: for we are members one of another. Be ye angry, and sin not: let not the sun go down upon your *63* wrath: neither give place to the devil.

"Let him that stole steal no more: but rather let him labour, working with his hands the thing which is good, that he may have to give to him that needeth.

"Let no corrupt communication proceed out of your mouth, but that which is good to the use of edifying, that it may minister grace unto the hearers.

"And grieve not the holy Spirit of God, whereby ye are sealed unto the day of redemption.

"Let all bitterness, and wrath, and anger, and clamour, and evil speaking, be put away from you, with all malice: and be ye kind one to another, tenderhearted, forgiving one another, even as God for Christ's sake hath forgiven you." (Ephesians 4:23-32.)

Paul taught that the priesthood is to be honored in the home, but the brethren must be examples of love and consideration:

"Be not drunk with wine, wherein is excess; but be filled with the Spirit; speaking to yourselves in psalms and hymns and spiritual songs, singing and making melody in your heart to the Lord; giving thanks always for all things unto God and the Father in the name of our Lord Jesus Christ; submitting yourselves one to another in the fear of God.

"Wives, submit yourselves unto your own husbands, as unto the Lord. For the husband is the head of the wife, even as Christ is the head of the church: and he is the saviour of the body. Therefore as the church is subject unto Christ, so let the wives be to their own husbands in every thing.

"Husbands, love your wives, even as Christ also loved the church, and gave himself for it; that he might sanctify and cleanse it with the washing of water by the word, that he might present it to himself a glorious church, not having spot, or wrinkle, or any such thing; but that it should be holy and without blemish.

"So ought men to love their wives as their own bodies. He that loveth his wife loveth himself. For no man ever yet hated his own flesh; but nourisheth and cherisheth it, even as the Lord the church: for we are members of his body, of his flesh, and of his bones.

"For this cause shall a man leave his father and mother, and shall be joined unto his wife, and they two shall be one flesh.

"This is a great mystery: but I speak concerning Christ and the church. Nevertheless let every one of you in particular so love his wife even as himself; and the wife see that she reverence her husband." (Ephesians 5:18-33.)

And what about the care of widows and orphans? Paul was most direct in the matter. Said he: "If any man or woman that believeth have widows, let them relieve them, and let not the church be charged; that it may relieve them that are widows indeed." (1 Timothy 5:16.)

He further explained:

"Honour widows that are widows indeed. But if any widow have children or nephews, let them learn first to shew piety at home, and to requite their parents: for that is good and acceptable before God.

"Now she that is a widow indeed, and desolate, trusteth in God, and continueth in supplications and prayers night and day. But she that liveth in pleasure is dead while she liveth. And these things give in charge, that they may be blameless.

"But if any provide not for his own, and specially for those of his own house, he hath denied the faith, and is worse than an infidel.

"Let not a widow be taken into the number under three-score years old, having been the wife of one man, well reported of for good works; if she have brought up children, if she have lodged strangers, if she have washed the saints' feet, if she have relieved the afflicted, if she have diligently followed every good work." (1 Timothy 5:3-10.)

However, of some younger ones he said: "But the
younger widows refuse: for when they have begun to wax
wanton against Christ, they will marry; having damnation, because they have cast off their first faith. And withal they learn
to be idle, wandering about from house to house; and not
only idle, but tattlers also and busybodies, speaking things
which they ought not." (1 Timothy 5:11-13.)

Surely this passage must reflect Paul's reaction to certain
cases he had observed personally, and that had disgusted
him, because of younger women in general he immediately
added: "I will therefore that the younger women marry, bear
children, guide the house, give none occasion to the adver-
sary to speak reproachfully. For some are already turned
aside after Satan." (1 Timothy 5:14-15.)

Isolated writings that seem to reveal unusual views on
marriage should be regarded only in the light of personal
opinion reflecting some specific difficult conditions facing
the Saints of Paul's day.

He spoke to the poor and urged them to live godly lives
"and having food and raiment . . . be therewith content."
(1 Timothy 6:8.) But to the rich he wrote as he gave direction
to Timothy:

"They that will be rich fall into temptation and a snare,
and into many foolish and hurtful lusts, which drown men in
destruction and perdition. For the love of money is the root
of all evil: which while some coveted after, they have erred
from the faith, and pierced themselves through with many
sorrows. . . .

"Charge them that are rich in this world, that they be not
highminded, nor trust in uncertain riches, but in the living
God, who giveth us richly all things to enjoy; that they do
good, that they be rich in good works, ready to distribute,
willing to communicate; laying up in store for themselves a
good foundation against the time to come, that they may lay
hold on eternal life." (1 Timothy 6:9-10; 17-19.)

In a strong appeal to Timothy, a minister for Christ, Paul
declared:

"But thou, O man of God, flee these things; and follow

after righteousness, godliness, faith, love, patience, meekness.

"Fight the good fight of faith, lay hold on eternal life, whereunto thou art also called, and hast professed a good profession before many witnesses.

"I give thee charge in the sight of God, who quickeneth all things, and before Christ Jesus, who before Pontius Pilate witnessed a good confession; that thou keep this commandment without spot, unrebukeable, until the appearing of our Lord Jesus Christ: which in his times he shall shew, who is the blessed and only Potentate, the King of kings, and Lord of lords; who only hath immortality, dwelling in the light which no man can approach unto; whom no man hath seen, nor can see: to whom be honour and power everlasting. . . .

"O Timothy, keep that which is committed to thy trust, avoiding profane and vain babblings, and oppositions of science falsely so called: which some professing have erred concerning the faith. Grace be with thee. Amen." (1 Timothy 6:11-16; 20-21.)

Paul loved Timothy as if he were his own son. He told him:

"Let no man despise thy youth; but be thou an example of the believers, in word, in conversation, in charity, in spirit, in faith, in purity. Till I come, give attendance to reading, to exhortation, to doctrine. Neglect not the gift that is in thee, which was given thee by prophecy, with the laying on of the hands of the presbytery.

"Meditate upon these things; give thyself wholly to them; that thy profiting may appear to all. Take heed unto thyself, and unto the doctrine; continue in them: for in doing this thou shalt both save thyself, and them that hear thee." (1 Timothy 4:12-16.)

And in regard to older brethren, Paul said, "Rebuke not an elder, but intreat him as a father; and younger men as brethren." (1 Timothy 5:1.) Then he urged Timothy to care for the widows and orphans. Did Paul know what James had written? James's epistle reads: "Pure religion and undefiled before God and the Father is this, To visit the fatherless and widows in their affliction, and to keep himself unspotted from the world." (James 1:27.)

Paul said further to Timothy:

"Let the elders that rule well be counted worthy of double honour, especially they who labour in the word and doctrine. For the scripture saith, Thou shalt not muzzle the ox that treadeth out the corn. And, The labourer is worthy of his reward.

"Against an elder receive not an accusation, but before two or three witnesses. Them that sin rebuke before all, that others also may fear.

"I charge thee before God, and the Lord Jesus Christ, and the elect angels, that thou observe these things without preferring one before another, doing nothing by partiality. Lay hands suddenly on no man, neither be partaker of other men's sins: keep thyself pure. . . .

"Some men's sins are open beforehand, going before to judgment; and some men they follow after. Likewise also the good works of some are manifest beforehand; and they that are otherwise cannot be hid." (1 Timothy 5:17-22, 24-25.)

And at another time Paul wrote to Timothy:

"Continue thou in the things which thou hast learned and hast been assured of, knowing of whom thou hast learned them; and that from a child thou hast known the holy scriptures, which are able to make thee wise unto salvation through faith which is in Christ Jesus.

"All scripture is given by inspiration of God, and is profitable for doctrine, for reproof, for correction, for instruction in righteousness: that the man of God may be perfect, throughly furnished unto all good works." (2 Timothy 3:14-17; see also James 1:22-25.)

Chapter Fourteen

THE PROBLEM
IN ROME

*P*AUL MET IMMORALITY of the Romans head on and with no excuses. He wrote to the Saints, saying, "I am ready to preach the gospel to you that are in Rome" and bore his testimony in doing so: "I am not ashamed of the gospel of Christ: for it is the power of God unto salvation to every one that believeth; to the Jew first, and also to the Greek. For therein is the righteousness of God revealed from faith to faith: as it is written, The just shall live by faith." (Romans 1:16-17.)

He had previously said: "Am I not an apostle? am I not free? have I not seen Jesus Christ our Lord? are not ye my work in the Lord?" (1 Corinthians 9:1.)

Paul knew whereof he spoke. But then he told the Romans that the wrath of God "is revealed from heaven against all ungodliness and unrighteousness of men, who hold the truth in unrighteousness; because that which may be known of God is manifest in them; for God hath shewed it unto them.

"For the invisible things of him from the creation of the world are clearly seen, being understood by the things that are made, even his eternal power and Godhead; so that they are without excuse." (Romans 1:18-20.)

Without reservation he launched into his attack on

moral corruption. He spoke of men who knew of God but did not honor Him:

"They glorified him not as God, neither were thankful; but became vain in their imaginations, and their foolish heart was darkened.

"Professing themselves to be wise, they became fools, and changed the glory of the uncorruptible God into an image made like to corruptible man, and to birds, and four-footed beasts, and creeping things.

"Wherefore God also gave them up to uncleanness through the lusts of their own hearts, to dishonour their own bodies between themselves: who changed the truth of God into a lie, and worshipped and served the creature more than the Creator, who is blessed for ever. Amen.

"For this cause God gave them up unto vile affections: for even their women did change the natural use into that which is against nature: and likewise also the men, leaving the natural use of the woman, burned in their lust one toward another; men with men working that which is unseemly, and receiving in themselves that recompence of their error which was meet.

"And even as they did not like to retain God in their knowledge, God gave them over to a reprobate mind, to do those things which are not convenient; being filled with all unrighteousness, fornication, wickedness, covetousness, maliciousness; full of envy, murder, debate, deceit, malignity; whisperers, backbiters, haters of God, despiteful, proud, boasters, inventors of evil things, disobedient to parents, without understanding, covenantbreakers, without natural affection, implacable, unmerciful: who knowing the judgment of God, that they which commit such things are worthy of death, not only do the same, but have pleasure in them that do them." (Romans 1:21-32.)

He had written the Corinthians in the same vein: "Be not deceived: neither fornicators, nor idolators, nor adulterers, nor effeminate, nor abusers of themselves with mankind, nor thieves, nor covetous, nor drunkards, nor revilers, nor extortioners, shall inherit the kingdom of God." (1 Corinthians 6:9-10.)

Here was fair warning: none such "shall inherit the kingdom of God."

This reminds us of what Moses taught on the same subject: "And if a man lie with his daughter in law, both of them shall surely be put to death: they have wrought confusion; their blood shall be upon them. If a man . . . lie with mankind, as he lieth with a woman, both of them have committed an abomination: they shall surely be put to death; their blood shall be upon them." (Leviticus 20:13.)

Moses also declared: "Thou shalt not lie with mankind, as with womankind: it is abomination." (Leviticus 18:22.) And in Deuteronomy he reemphasized his teaching: "There shall be no whore of the daughters of Israel, nor a sodomite of the sons of Israel." (Deuteronomy 23:17.)

The advice of the Lord has ever been: "Be ye clean, that bear the vessels of the Lord." (Isaiah 52:11.)

Chapter Fifteen

DISCOURSE ON FAITH

*P*AUL TAUGHT FAITH and works, but he made it clear that faith is the element from which good works grow. His discourse on faith is one of the classics in all scripture, not only teaching this great principle, but also revealing how well read he was in the scriptures and how fully he knew of the tremendous faith that motivated the ancients. This discourse appears in the eleventh chapter of his letter to the Hebrews and should be read in full there.

Every lover of Paul teaches his definition of faith: "Faith is the substance of things hoped for, the evidence of things not seen." (Hebrews 11:1.)

Continuing, he goes through a list of the ancients, showing how each one achieved through faith in God.

Paul did not forget the Creation; he dealt with it at the beginning of his discourse: "Through faith we understand that the worlds were framed by the word of God, so that things which are seen were not made of things which do appear." (Hebrews 11:3.)

Here we have one more affirmation of the divine origin of the earth.

Paul's mention of "the word of God" calls to mind John's writings: "In the beginning was the Word, and the Word was with God, and the Word was God. The same was in the beginning with God. All things were made by him; and without him was not any thing made that was made." (John 1:1-3.)

It reminds us, too, that Paul himself had written to the saints concerning the Creation. (See Hebrews 1:1-3; Colossians 1:13-18.) Does the translation of "the word of God" in Paul's writings refer personally to the Savior as the Creator? Or could it mean that as God gave the verbal orders, creation was brought about? Either or both could be true.

Paul refers to Abel and his "more excellent sacrifice," and to Enoch, who "was translated that he should not see death." (Hebrews 11:4-5.)

He provides us with this choice verse: "Without faith it is impossible to please him: for he that cometh to God must believe that he is, and that he is a rewarder of them that diligently seek him." (Hebrews 11:6.)

He speaks of Abraham's great faith:

"By faith Abraham, when he was called to go out into a place which he should after receive for an inheritance, obeyed; and he went out, not knowing whither he went.

"By faith he sojourned in the land of promise, as in a strange country, dwelling in tabernacles with Isaac and Jacob, the heirs with him of the same promise: for he looked for a city which hath foundations, whose builder and maker is God.

"Through faith also Sara herself received strength to conceive seed, and was delivered of a child when she was past age, because she judged him faithful who had promised.

"Therefore sprang there even of one, and him as good as dead, so many as the stars of the sky in multitude, and as the sand which is by the sea shore innumerable." (Hebrews 11:8-12.)

Continuing with Abraham, Paul writes further: "By faith Abraham, when he was tried, offered up Isaac: and he that had received the promises offered up his only begotten son, of whom it was said, That in Isaac shall thy seed be called: accounting that God was able to raise him up, even from the dead; from whence also he received him in a figure." (Abraham 11:17-19.)

Isaac, Jacob, and Esau are mentioned, as is Joseph who was sold into Egypt.

Paul has even more to say about Moses' faith:

"By faith Moses, when he was born, was hid three months of his parents, because they saw he was a proper child; and they were not afraid of the king's commandment.

"By faith Moses, when he was come to years, refused to be called the son of Pharaoh's daughter; choosing rather to suffer affliction with the people of God, than to enjoy the pleasures of sin for a season; esteeming the reproach of Christ greater riches than the treasures in Egypt: for he had respect unto the recompence of the reward.

"By faith he forsook Egypt, not fearing the wrath of the king: for he endured, as seeing him who is invisible.

"Through faith he kept the passover, and the sprinkling of blood, lest he that destroyed the firstborn should touch them.

"By faith they passed through the Red sea as by dry land: which the Egyptians assaying to do were drowned." (Hebrews 11:23-29.)

The fall of Jericho—was it fact or fiction? Paul cites it as fact in verse 30.

He speaks of the accomplishment but also the sacrifices of the ancient Saints, "who through faith subdued kingdoms, wrought righteousness, obtained promises, stopped the mouths of lions, quenched the violence of fire, escaped the edge of the sword, out of weakness were made strong, waxed valiant in fight, turned to flight the armies of the aliens.

"Women received their dead raised to life again: and others were tortured, not accepting deliverance; that they might obtain a better resurrection: and others had trial of cruel mockings and scourgings, yea, moreover of bonds and imprisonment: they were stoned, they were sawn asunder, were tempted, were slain with the sword: they wandered about in sheepskins and goatskins; being destitute, afflicted, tormented; (of whom the world was not worthy:) they wandered in deserts, and in mountains, and in dens and caves of the earth.

"And these all, having obtained a good report through faith, received not the promise: God having provided some better thing for us, that they without us should not be made perfect." (Hebrews 11:33-40.)

Doesn't this demonstrate an understanding of the required relationships for all generations, and the responsibility of the living toward the dead?

Chapter Sixteen

PAUL'S CLASSIC WRITING

*P*AUL WROTE three great classic passages—his sermon on faith, which was discussed in chapter 15, his sermon on charity, and his sermon on the resurrection. The best known, of course, is his dissertation on charity in the thirteenth chapter of 1 Corinthians:

"Though I speak with the tongues of men and of angels, and have not charity, I am become as sounding brass, or a tinkling cymbal.

"And though I have the gift of prophecy, and understand all mysteries, and all knowledge; and though I have all faith, so that I could remove mountains, and have not charity, I am nothing.

"And though I bestow all my goods to feed the poor, and though I give my body to be burned, and have not charity, it profiteth me nothing.

"Charity suffereth long, and is kind; charity envieth not; charity vaunteth not itself, is not puffed up, doth not behave itself unseemly, seeketh not her own, is not easily provoked, thinketh no evil; rejoiceth not in iniquity, but rejoiceth in the truth; beareth all things, believeth all things, hopeth all things, endureth all things.

"Charity never faileth: but whether there be prophecies, they shall fail; whether there be tongues, they shall cease; whether there be knowledge, it shall vanish away."

As we ponder these words we must also complete the reading:

"For we know in part, and we prophesy in part. But when that which is perfect is come, then that which is in part shall be done away.

"When I was a child, I spake as a child, I understood as a child, I thought as a child: but when I became a man, I put away childish things.

"For now we see through a glass, darkly; but then face to face: now I know in part; but then shall I know even as also I am known.

"And now abideth faith, hope, charity, these three; but the greatest of these is charity." (1 Corinthians 13:1-13.)

Yes, charity, the pure love of Christ! There is nothing to compare with it.

Think of the Savior and His teachings concerning love. He gave us this wonderful promise:

"He that hath my commandments, and keepeth them, he it is that loveth me: and he that loveth me shall be loved of my Father, and I will love him, and will manifest myself to him. . . .

"If a man love me, he will keep my words: and my Father will love him, and we will come unto him, and make our abode with him.

"He that loveth me not keepeth not my sayings: and the word which ye hear is not mine, but the Father's which sent me." (John 14:21, 23-24.)

He also taught the message that Jesus had given when the lawyer asked Him, "Master, which is the great commandment in the law?

"Jesus said unto him, Thou shalt love the Lord thy God with all thy heart, and with all thy soul, and with all thy mind.

"This is the first and great commandment.

"And the second is like unto it, Thou shalt love thy neighbour as thyself.

"On these two commandments hang all the law and the prophets." (Matthew 22:34-40.)

How all-inclusive: "On these two commandments hang all the law and the prophets." All! The whole gospel plan! Without the love of Christ, what would we have? Truly, "the greatest of these is love," as later translations express it.

The second classic is Paul's discourse on faith, discussed in the previous chapter. And the third, which stands out in all scripture, is Paul's defense of the resurrection in the fifteenth chapter of 1 Corinthians: "Now is Christ risen from the dead, and become the firstfruits of them that slept. For since by man came death, by man came also the resurrection of the dead. For as in Adam all die, even so in Christ shall all be made alive." (1 Corinthians 15:20-22.)

It is in this great epistle to the Corinthians that Paul speaks of vicarious baptism for the dead. As one of his proofs of the fact of the resurrection, he asks: "Else what shall they do which are baptized for the dead, if the dead rise not at all? why are they then baptized for the dead?" (1 Corinthians 15:29.)

This statement is well sustained by modern translations of the Bible. For example, *The Authentic New Testament* by Schonfield reads: "What are they doing who are immersed on behalf of the dead? If the dead are not raised, why be immersed on their behalf?"

The New English Bible states: "Again there are those who receive baptism on behalf of the dead. Why should they do this? If the dead are not raised to life at all, what do they mean by being baptized on their behalf?"

The *New American Bible*, a Roman Catholic publication, gives this rendering: "If the dead are not raised, what about those who have themselves baptized on behalf of the dead? If the raising of the dead is not a reality, why be baptized on their behalf?"

Other Bible translations, new and old, carry this important verse in much the same language.

Paul understood the reason for baptism and that it was a universal requirement of all who could believe and repent, not even excluding the dead. As an apostle of Jesus Christ, would he not know as well as Peter that Jesus preached to the dead while His body lay in the tomb? (1 Peter 3:18-20; 4:6; John 5:25, 28-29.)

Paul's discussion of the three degrees of glory is enlightening:

"There are . . . celestial bodies, and bodies terrestrial: but the glory of the celestial is one, and the glory of the terrestrial is another.

"There is one glory of the sun, and another glory of the moon, and another glory of the stars: for one star differeth from another star in glory.

"So also is the resurrection of the dead. It is sown in corruption; it is raised in incorruption: it is sown in dishonour; it is raised in glory: it is sown in weakness; it is raised in power: it is sown a natural body; it is raised a spiritual body. There is a natural body, and there is a spiritual body." (1 Corinthians 15:40-44.)

The Savior had said that in His Father's house are many mansions. (John 14:2.) He also taught that we shall be judged by our works. No wonder Paul said that as "one star differeth from another star in glory, so also is the resurrection of the dead." (1 Corinthians 15:41-42.)

Then Paul wrote this great climax to his resurrection treatise: "Death is swallowed up in victory. O death, where is thy sting? O grave, where is thy victory?" (1 Corinthians 15:54-55.)

Chapter Seventeen

THE ARMOR OF GOD

*P*AUL URGED THE SAINTS to "be not conformed to this world" (Romans 12:2), and he stressed throughout his labors the importance of this teaching. In describing the Christian way to live, he declared to the Romans:

"Let love be without dissimulation. Abhor that which is evil; cleave to that which is good.

"Be kindly affectioned one to another with brotherly love; in honour preferring one another; not slothful in business; fervent in spirit; serving the Lord; rejoicing in hope; patient in tribulation; continuing instant in prayer; distributing to the necessity of saints; given to hospitality.

"Bless them which persecute you: bless, and curse not.

"Rejoice with them that do rejoice, and weep with them that weep.

"Be of the same mind one toward another. Mind not high things, but condescend to men of low estate. Be not wise in your own conceits.

"Recompense to no man evil for evil. Provide things honest in the sight of all men.

"If it be possible, as much as lieth in you, live peaceably with all men.

"Dearly beloved, avenge not yourselves, but rather give place unto wrath: for it is written, Vengeance is mine; I will repay, saith the Lord.

"Therefore if thine enemy hunger, feed him; if he thirst, give him drink: for in so doing thou shalt heap coals of fire on his head.

"Be not overcome of evil, but overcome evil with good." (Romans 12:9-21.)

Paul taught these Romans to respect those who were in authority over them:

"Let every soul be subject unto the higher powers. For there is no power but of God: the powers that be are ordained of God.

"Whosoever therefore resisteth the power, resisteth the ordinance of God: and they that resist shall receive to themselves damnation.

"For rulers are not a terror to good works, but to the evil. Wilt thou then not be afraid of the power? do that which is good, and thou shalt have praise of the same: for he is the minister of God to thee for good. But if thou do that which is evil, be afraid; for he beareth not the sword in vain: for he is the minister of God, a revenger to execute wrath upon him that doeth evil.

"Wherefore ye must needs be subject, not only for wrath, but also for conscience sake.

"For for this cause pay ye tribute also: for they are God's ministers, attending continually upon this very thing." (Romans 13:1-6.)

And then as he spoke further of the relationships of the Saints, he wrote:

"Render therefore to all their dues: tribute to whom tribute is due; custom to whom custom; fear to whom fear; honour to whom honour.

"Owe no man any thing, but to love one another: for he that loveth another hath fulfilled the law.

"For this, Thou shalt not commit adultery, Thou shalt not kill, Thou shalt not steal, Thou shalt not bear false witness, Thou shalt not covet; and if there be any other commandment, it is briefly comprehended in this saying, namely, Thou shalt love thy neighbour as thyself.

"Love worketh no ill to his neighbour: therefore love is the fulfilling of the law." (Romans 13:7-10.)

This great apostle also renewed one of Christ's vital teachings from the Sermon on the Mount, in which the Lord said: "Judge not, that ye be not judged." (Matthew 7:1.) Paul wrote:

"Why dost thou judge thy brother? or why dost thou set at nought thy brother? for we shall all stand before the judgment seat of Christ.

"For it is written, As I live, saith the Lord, every knee shall bow to me, and every tongue shall confess to God. So then every one of us shall give account of himself to God.

"Let us not therefore judge one another any more: but judge this rather, that no man put a stumblingblock or an occasion to fall in his brother's way." (Romans 14:10-13.)

Again he cautioned: "It is good neither to eat flesh, nor to drink wine, nor any thing whereby thy brother stumbleth, or is offended, or is made weak." (Romans 14:21.)

This reflected what he had told the Corinthians:

"Take heed lest by any means this liberty of yours become a stumblingblock to them that are weak.

"For if any man see thee which hast knowledge sit at meat in the idol's temple, shall not the conscience of him which is weak be emboldened to eat those things which are offered to idols; and through thy knowledge shall the weak brother perish, for whom Christ died?

"But when ye sin so against the brethren, and wound their weak conscience, ye sin against Christ.

"Wherefore, if meat make my brother to offend, I will eat no flesh while the world standeth, lest I make my brother to offend." (1 Corinthians 8:9-13.)

In his appeal for righteous living Paul gave us this priceless passage:

"Be strong in the Lord, and in the power of his might.

"Put on the whole armour of God, that ye may be able to stand against the wiles of the devil.

"For we wrestle not against flesh and blood, but against principalities, against powers, against the rulers of the darkness of this world, against spiritual wickedness in high places.

"Wherefore take unto you the whole armour of God, that ye may be able to withstand in the evil day, and having done all, to stand.

"Stand therefore, having your loins girt about with truth, and having on the breastplate of righteousness; and your feet shod with the preparation of the gospel of peace; above all, taking the shield of faith, wherewith ye shall be able to quench all the fiery darts of the wicked.

"And take the helmet of salvation, and the sword of the Spirit, which is the word of God: praying always with all prayer and supplication in the Spirit, and watching thereunto with all perseverance and supplication for all saints." (Ephesians 6:10-18.)

How colorful are Paul's lessons! How easy to understand!

Chapter Eighteen

M E L C H I Z E D E K

O F   S A L E M

*P*AUL OBVIOUSLY KNEW a great deal about Melchizedek and the priesthood that was named after him, information that is not available elsewhere in the scriptures. The fifth chapter of Hebrews contains these very important passages:

"Every high priest taken from among men is ordained for men in things pertaining to God, that he may offer both gifts and sacrifices for sins: who can have compassion on the ignorant, and on them that are out of the way; for that he himself also is compassed with infirmity. And by reason hereof he ought, as for the people, so also for himself, to offer for sins.

"And no man taketh this honour unto himself, but he that is called of God, as was Aaron. So also Christ glorified not himself to be made an high priest; but he that said unto him, Thou art my Son, to day have I begotten thee. As he saith also in another place, Thou art a priest for ever after the order of Melchisedec." (Hebrews 5:1-6.)

Then Paul added this beautiful thought concerning Christ: "Though he were a Son, yet learned he obedience by the things which he suffered; and being made perfect, he became the author of eternal salvation unto all them that obey him; called of God an high priest after the order of Melchisedec." (Hebrews 5:8-10.)

Again speaking of the Savior, Paul continues: ". . . whither the forerunner is for us entered, even Jesus, made an high priest for ever after the order of Melchisedec." (Hebrews 6:20.)

Then he resumes, apparently knowing full well the identity of that great king of Salem:

"For this Melchisedec, king of Salem, priest of the most high God, who met Abraham returning from the slaughter of the kings, and blessed him; to whom also Abraham gave a tenth part of all; first being by interpretation King of righteousness, and after that also King of Salem, which is, King of peace; without father, without mother, without descent, having neither beginning of days, nor end of life; but made like unto the Son of God; abideth a priest continually.

"Now consider how great this man was, unto whom even the patriarch Abraham gave the tenth of the spoils.

"And verily they that are of the sons of Levi, who receive the office of the priesthood, have a commandment to take tithes of the people according to the law, that is, of their brethren, though they come out of the loins of Abraham: but he whose descent is not counted from them received tithes of Abraham, and blessed him that had the promises. And without all contradiction the less is blessed of the better.

"And here men that die receive tithes; but there he receiveth them, of whom it is witnessed that he liveth.

"And as I may so say, Levi also, who receiveth tithes, payed tithes in Abraham. For he was yet in the loins of his father, when Melchisedec met him.

"If therefore perfection were by the Levitical priesthood, (for under it the people received the law,) what further need was there that another priest should rise after the order of Melchisedec, and not be called after the order of Aaron? For the priesthood being changed, there is made of necessity a change also of the law. For he of whom these things are spoken pertaineth to another tribe, of which no man gave attendance at the altar.

"For it is evident that our Lord sprang out of Juda; of which tribe Moses spake nothing concerning priesthood. And it is yet far more evident: for that after the similitude of Melchisedec there ariseth another priest, who is made, not after the law of a carnal commandment, but after the power of an endless life. For he testifieth, Thou art a priest for ever after the order of Melchisedec.

"For there is verily a disannulling of the commandment going before for the weakness and unprofitableness thereof. For the law made nothing perfect, but the bringing in of a better hope did; by the which we draw nigh unto God.

"And inasmuch as not without an oath he was made priest: (for those priests were made without an oath; but this with an oath by him that said unto him, The Lord sware and will not repent, Thou art a priest for ever after the order of Melchisedec:) by so much was Jesus made a surety of a better testament." (Hebrews 7:1-22.)

Melchizedek is mentioned also in Genesis, of course. It was he to whom Abraham paid tithes. (Genesis 14:18-20.) David spoke of him in Psalms: "The Lord hath sworn, and will not repent, Thou art a priest for ever after the order of Melchizedek." (Psalms 110:4.)

It was in this same psalm that David referred to Christ: "The Lord said unto my Lord, Sit thou at my right hand, until I make thine enemies thy footstool." (Psalms 110:1.)

Chapter Nineteen

PAUL WAS

AN APOSTLE

WRITING TO THE WAVERING Corinthians who seemed to doubt his teachings, Paul declared: "Am I not an apostle? am I not free? have I not seen Jesus Christ our Lord? are not ye my work in the Lord? If I be not an apostle unto others, yet doubtless I am to you: for the seal of mine apostleship are ye in the Lord." (1 Corinthians 9:1-2.)

And indeed he had seen the Lord, as Ananias himself testified. (Acts 9:17.)

But there was another time. Paul wrote that the resurrected Savior "was seen of James; then of all the apostles. And last of all he was seen of me also, as of one born out of due time." (1 Corinthians 15:7-8.)

Paul is first called an apostle in the fourteenth chapter of Acts: "The multitude of the city was divided: and part held with the Jews, and part with the apostles. . . . Which when the apostles, Barnabas and Paul, heard of, they rent their clothes, and ran in among the people, crying out." (Acts 14:4, 14.) This event, of course, followed the call from the Holy Ghost as recorded in Acts 13.

Paul seems to have taken righteous pride in his call, since he spoke of it so often.

To the Romans he wrote: "Paul, a servant of Jesus Christ,
called to be an apostle, separated unto the gospel of God."
(Romans 1:1.) "Lord, they have killed thy prophets, and digged down thine altars; and I am left alone, and they seek my life." (Romans 11:3.)

Paul Was an Apostle

He urged Timothy: "Be not thou . . . ashamed of the testimony of our Lord, nor of me his prisoner: but be thou partaker of the afflictions of the gospel according to the power of God; who hath saved us, and called us with an holy calling, not according to our works, but according to his own purpose and grace, which was given us in Christ Jesus before the world began, but is now made manifest by the appearing of our Saviour Jesus Christ, who hath abolished death, and hath brought life and immortality to light through the gospel: whereunto I am appointed a preacher, and an apostle, and a teacher of the Gentiles." (2 Timothy 1:8-11.)

87

Writing the Corinthians, he identified himself as "Paul, called to be an apostle of Jesus Christ through the will of God." (1 Corinthians 1:1.)

In his second letter to the Corinthians he declares himself to be "Paul, an apostle of Jesus Christ by the will of God, and Timothy our brother, unto the church of God which is at Corinth, with all the saints which are in all Achaia." (2 Corinthians 1:1.)

He did likewise in writing to the Galatians, Ephesians, Colossians, and others.

To Timothy, he wrote that he was "an apostle of Jesus Christ by the commandment of God our Saviour, and Lord Jesus Christ, which is our hope." (1 Timothy 1:1.) "Whereunto I am ordained a preacher, and an apostle, (I speak the truth in Christ, and lie not;) a teacher of the Gentiles in faith and verity." (1 Timothy 2:7.)

To Titus, he wrote that he was "a servant of God, and an apostle of Jesus Christ, according to the faith of God's elect, and the acknowledging of the truth which is after godliness." (Titus 1:1.)

The calling was mighty, and Paul recognized this fact in regard to others of the Twelve. He called himself the least of them because he had persecuted the church: "I am the least of the apostles, that am not meet to be called an apostle, because I persecuted the church of God. But by the grace of God I am what I am: and his grace which was bestowed upon me was not in vain; but I laboured more abundantly than they all: yet not I, but the grace of God which was with me." (1 Corinthians 15:9-10.)

Obviously, then, the pride he felt in his calling was a humble sense of gratitude, because all his life he deeply regretted the persecutions of his earlier years. But as he told the Romans, he was not in any way ashamed of the gospel (Romans 1:16), but rather he rejoiced in it. He glorified both God and Christ, not taking any glory to himself. (Romans 4:20; 11:36; 16:27.)

Taking no honor to himself, Paul gave God the credit for all that he did. He taught: "God is not the author of confusion, but of peace, as in all churches of the saints." (1 Corinthians 14:33.)

He suffered tremendously in his work: "Persecutions, afflictions, which came unto me at Antioch, at Iconium, at Lystra; what persecutions I endured: but out of them all the Lord delivered me. . . . The Lord stood with me, and strengthened me; that by me the preaching might be fully known, and that all the Gentiles might hear: and I was delivered out of the mouth of the lion." (2 Timothy 3:11; 4:17.)

Summarizing further afflictions, he declared: "Of the Jews five times received I forty stripes save one. Thrice was I beaten with rods, once was I stoned, thrice I suffered shipwreck, a night and a day I have been in the deep; in journeyings often, in perils of waters, in perils of robbers, in perils by mine own countrymen, in perils by the heathen, in perils in the city, in perils in the wilderness, in perils in the sea, in perils among false brethren; in weariness and painfulness, in watchings often, in hunger and thirst, in fastings often, in cold and nakedness." (2 Corinthians 11:24-27.)

Can one wonder that to Timothy he wrote his final letter from his imprisonment in Rome, very much as a benediction on his life? The *New Analytical Bible and Dictionary of the*

Bible (p. 1378) speaks of this period in Paul's life, describing the persecution in Rome that led to his final letter to Timothy:

"One of the victims of this persecution was the Apostle Paul. He was brought to Rome and imprisoned a second time. It was during this imprisonment, awaiting his death, which was probably 67 or 68 A.D., that he wrote his last epistle, the Second Epistle to Timothy.

"He tells that he is living in the expectation of being 'offered up,' but through it all is the note of Christian triumph, the statement of a man who knows Whom he has believed and to Whom he is committed in his life and his death."

And so Paul wrote his benediction, the words of one of God's greatest noblemen: I am now ready to be offered, and the time of my departure is at hand. I have fought a good fight, I have finished my course, I have kept the faith: henceforth there is laid up for me a crown of righteousness, which the Lord, the righteous judge, shall give me at that day: and not to me only, but unto all them also that love his appearing." (2 Timothy 4:6-8.)

INDEX